THEORY OF EVERYTHING

A JOURNEY BEYOND THE KNOWN

THEORY OF EVERYTHING

A JOURNEY BEYOND THE KNOWN

SANCHIT MATHUR

PAPER TOWNS
PUBLISHERS

PAPER TOWNS
PUBLISHERS

First published by

Papertowns Publishers
72, Vishwanath Dham Colony,
Niwaru Road, Jhotwara,
Jaipur, 302012

Theory of Everything: A Journey Beyond The Known

ISBN Print Book – 978-93-6185-225-1

Cover Designed by: Sanchit Mathur

Printed in India

Description

The world you see is only a fraction of what exists..

Theory of Everything uncovers the hidden layers of reality where intuition whispers, timelines shift, and parallel possibilities coexist. Step into a journey that bridges science and spirituality. Learn how to navigate these unseen currents, harness your mind's extraordinary power, and step fully into a life of insight, purpose, and infinite potential.

CONTENTS

INTRODUCTION

PART 1: THE POWER OF THE MIND

PART 2: THE NATURE OF REALITY

PART 3: HARNESSING ENERGY AND MANIFESTATION

PART 4: BEYOND THE PHYSICAL

PART 5: TRANSFORMATION AND PURPOSE

CONCLUSION

INTRODUCTION

Chapter 1

A Journey Beyond the Known

What if the world you see around you is only half the story? What if the answers to your deepest questions about success, happiness, and purpose aren't scattered somewhere out there, but hidden within you?

From the ancient teachings of mystics to the groundbreaking discoveries of modern science, one thing becomes clear: the potential within us is vast, mysterious, and largely undiscovered.

We live in a world that often glorifies logic, tangible results, and visible progress. Yet, some of the most life-altering experiences are intangible - moments of insight, intuition, or a sudden sense of connection with something larger than ourselves. These experiences whisper of unseen forces and untapped realms within the mind, urging us to look beyond the ordinary and explore the extraordinary.

Life is full of questions: *Why am I here? What's my purpose? Why do certain things feel like they're meant to be?* We search for answers in books, relationships, careers, and even in the stars. But, what if the most of these truths lie within?

Every great discovery, invention, or idea began with a single spark - a thought, a hunch, or even a dream. But where do these flashes of brilliance come from? Is it just a random chance, or could it be a glimpse into something deeper, a hidden realm within us?

The truth is, there's more to reality than meets the eye. Think of those moments when time seems to slow down, when a sudden intuition saves the day, or when a vivid dream feels like a message from another world. These experiences aren't just coincidences, they're clues; hints that there's a vast, interconnected web of energy and consciousness shaping our lives. And, you're not just a passive observer of this web, you're a creator within it.

Every thought you have is more than just a fleeting mental event; it's a powerful force that ripples outwards, shaping your reality in ways you might not even realize. When we toss a pebble into a still pond, the ripples expand, changing the surface of the water. In the same way, your thoughts ripple through your life, influencing your emotions, decisions, and even the circumstances you encounter.

Science calls this neuroplasticity. It's the brain's incredible ability to reorganize and rewire itself based on your thoughts, beliefs, and experiences. Every time you focus on a positive thought, repeat an empowering affirmation, or visualize a desired outcome, you're physically reshaping your brain, laying down new neural pathways that can transform your life. Ancient wisdom called it the law of cause and effect.

Also, have you ever heard of the placebo effect? It's a scientific marvel that proves the power of belief. People given sugar pills instead of real medicine often show real improvement, simply because they believe they're being treated. Now imagine if you could harness that power intentionally to heal, to grow, to thrive.

For centuries, science and spirituality seemed to speak different languages. But today, they're converging in astonishing ways. Science dealt with facts, measurements, and tangible results, while spirituality explored the unseen, the intuitive, and the deeply personal.

Quantum physics reveals a universe where particles can be in two places at once, where observation changes outcomes, and where everything is interconnected at a fundamental level. Sounds familiar? These aren't just abstract scientific concepts; they echo the teachings of ancient mystics and sages who spoke of a unified field of existence, a world where thoughts and energy flow together seamlessly.

Take meditation, for example. Once dismissed as a religious practice, it's now a scientifically proven method for reducing stress, enhancing creativity, and even rewiring the brain. It's as if the ancient wisdom of sages and the data-driven insights of modern researchers are finally joining forces to reveal just how powerful the mind truly is.

Picture yourself holding a key to a door you've never dared to open. On the other side lies a world of infinite possibilities. A world where your thoughts shape reality, where your dreams become blueprints for success, and where the answers to your biggest questions and life's greatest mysteries are within reach.

This isn't just another book with a collection of theories or promises of self-help; this book has answers to a few of those questions which have never been answered before. Your way of looking at things may change from the moment you start reading it.

Imagine those moments in life when you've felt a sudden spark of insight, a strange coincidence, or a gut feeling that steered you in the right direction. These aren't random, they're glimpses of a deeper reality at play. The journey we're about to take is about understanding and harnessing that deeper reality.

Think of this book as a map and a guide. It won't just tell you about the treasures hidden within your subconscious mind, it will show you how to find them, how to unlock them, and how to use them to create the life you've always dreamed of. Each chapter will help you peel back the layers of your mind, revealing truths that will change the way you see yourself and the world.

You'll explore the hidden powers of your subconscious, learn to harness the energy of your thoughts, and discover how to align your inner world with the outer life you desire. This isn't about magic or shortcuts; it's about understanding the principles that shape your reality and learning to use them intentionally.

The first step is the hardest, but it's also the most rewarding. Are you ready to discover the infinite potential within you?

The world beyond the known is waiting.

PART 1

The Power of the Mind

Chapter 2

The Subconscious Mind (The Hidden Architect of Your Life)

Imagine waking up in the morning and brushing your teeth without a second thought, or instinctively stepping on the brake when a car suddenly stops ahead of you. Have you ever wondered how you perform these actions effortlessly?

And, why do certain habits feel impossible to break or certain fears persist even when you know they're irrational?

This is the work of your subconscious mind; a powerful yet often overlooked force that operates beneath the surface of your awareness. It's a vast, hidden system that governs your thoughts, behaviors, and even your physical health.

While your conscious mind is your moment-to-moment awareness, your subconscious mind works silently in the background, storing memories, shaping beliefs, and driving automatic behaviors that influence nearly every aspect of your life.

The subconscious mind is like the engine room of a ship. It silently powers your life, steering your decisions, habits, and emotions without requiring your conscious input. While your conscious mind focuses on immediate tasks like planning your day or solving a problem, your subconscious mind quietly runs the deeper programs that shape your behaviors, reactions, and even your sense of identity.

From mundane daily routines, like brushing your teeth, to profound life choices, such as career paths and relationships, the subconscious is your unseen navigator. It operates on autopilot, executing mental programs you've accumulated over your lifetime. These programs, whether empowering or limiting, play a crucial role in shaping the trajectory of your life.

Conscious vs. Subconscious Mind

To better understand the relationship between your conscious and subconscious mind, imagine an iceberg floating in the ocean. The visible part above the waterline represents your conscious mind, where logical thinking, decision-making, and will-power reside. This is the realm of your immediate awareness. The part of you that analyzes situations and solves problems.

But below the surface lies the massive, hidden portion of the iceberg: your subconscious mind. This is where your long-term memories, deeply ingrained beliefs, emotional reactions, and habitual patterns are stored. It's a vast reservoir of information and experiences, many of which were absorbed during your early years when your mind was highly impressionable. Scientists estimate that up to 95% of your daily actions and decisions are influenced by your subconscious.

Research suggests that your subconscious mind processes about 11 million bits of information per second, compared to the 40 to 50 bits handled by your conscious mind. This disparity highlights just how much of your life is influenced by the subconscious.

Think back to your childhood. How did your environment shape you? Did your caregivers encourage and uplift you, or were you met with criticism and doubt? During your formative years, your brain operated predominantly in a theta brainwave state, a highly suggestible frequency that allowed you to absorb information like a sponge. This state was ideal for learning but also made you vulnerable to negative programming.

If you were told, "You're so smart!" your subconscious likely internalized a belief in your capability. But if you repeatedly heard, "You'll never amount to anything", that harmful message may have rooted itself deeply, influencing your self-esteem and limiting your potential as an adult.

The subconscious mind doesn't evaluate or question the information it receives; it simply records and stores it. These stored messages become the foundation for your thoughts, emotions, and behaviors later in life.

Your subconscious mind doesn't merely store information, it actively shapes your perception of reality. Here is how it works:

- **Belief Filters:** Your subconscious beliefs act like filters through which you interpret the world. If you believe you're unworthy of love, you may unconsciously sabotage relationships or ignore signs of affection. On the other hand, if you believe you're capable and deserving, you're more likely to pursue opportunities and take-up challenges with confidence.
- **Emotional Triggers:** The subconscious holds emotional memories, which can trigger automatic responses in the present. For example, if you were scolded for making mistakes as a child, you might feel a disproportionate sense of fear or shame when you make an error as an adult.
- **Behavioral Patterns:** Many of your daily actions, from how you respond to stress to how you interact with others, are driven by subconscious programming. This is why changing habits can feel so challenging. Your subconscious mind is wired to maintain the status quo, even if it's not serving your best interests.

The Reticular Activating System (Your Mind's Gatekeeper)

The Reticular Activating System (RAS) is a network of neurons in your brainstem that plays a crucial role in determining what information your brain pays attention to. Since your senses are bombarded with millions of stimuli every second, the RAS helps filter this data, prioritizing what aligns with your subconscious beliefs and current focus.

For example, if you decide to buy a red car, you suddenly start noticing red cars everywhere. They were always there, but your RAS now highlights them because they've become relevant to you. Similarly, if you believe "I'm not good at public speaking," your RAS will focus on instances that reinforce this belief, making it feel even more true.

This selective attention system means that by changing your subconscious beliefs, you can reprogram your RAS to focus on opportunities, solutions, and positive outcomes instead of reinforcing limiting narratives.

Habits: The Subconscious Autopilot

Your subconscious mind thrives on efficiency, which is why it automates repetitive behaviors in the form of habits. Habits are like well-worn paths in a forest; once established, they're easy to follow.

Consider how you learned to drive a car. Initially, every action required conscious effort: adjusting mirrors, checking blind spots, coordinating pedals. Over time, these actions became automatic, thanks to your subconscious.

But this automation applies to emotional and mental habits too. If you've developed a habit of self-doubt or overthinking, these patterns become ingrained, running on autopilot unless consciously addressed.

To change your life, you must first change the beliefs and habits stored in your subconscious mind. The good thing is that the subconscious is malleable. It can be reprogrammed with the right tools and consistent effort.

Start by identifying limiting beliefs. These often manifest as recurring negative thoughts or patterns, such as "I'm not good enough" or "Success is only for other people." Once you're aware of these beliefs, challenge them. Ask yourself: "Is this belief objectively true? Where did it come from? How has it served me, and is it time to let it go?"

Replace limiting beliefs with empowering ones through affirmations, visualization, and consistent practice. For instance, if you want to cultivate confidence, repeat affirmations like "I am capable and deserving of success" daily, and visualize yourself succeeding in various scenarios.

Don't worry if you don't know about these techniques yet, they will be discussed in detail in the upcoming chapters.

The Placebo Effect: Proof of the Subconscious Mind's Power

The placebo effect is a stunning example of how your subconscious beliefs can directly impact your physical reality. In medical studies, patients who believe they're receiving effective treatment, when in fact they're given a sugar pill-often show real improvements in their condition.

This demonstrates the mind's extraordinary ability to influence the body. If belief alone can trigger healing, imagine the transformative potential of intentionally aligning your subconscious mind with your goals.

Practical Tools for Reprogramming Your Subconscious

1. **Visualization:** Spend a few minutes each day vividly imagining your desired outcomes. Picture yourself living the life you want, engaging all your senses to make the experience as real as possible.
2. **Affirmations:** Repeat positive statements that reinforce the beliefs you want to instill. For example, "I am worthy of love and success" or "I attract opportunities effortlessly."
3. **Meditation:** Use meditation to quiet your conscious mind and access deeper layers of your subconscious. Guided meditations focused on reprogramming beliefs can be especially effective.

4. **Journaling:** Write down your thoughts, goals, and affirmations to solidify your intentions and track your progress.
5. **Hypnosis:** Hypnotherapy can bypass the critical filter of the conscious mind, allowing direct access to the subconscious for deeper reprogramming. (Only performed by experts and professionals in extreme cases. Not recommended for daily/personal use.)

The subconscious mind is like fertile soil, ready to grow whatever seeds you plant. The key is to plant the right seeds of positive thoughts, empowering beliefs, and constructive habits. By consciously working to align your subconscious programming with your goals and desires, you can transform your life from the inside out.

Remember, your subconscious is always working, whether you guide it or not. Why not take the reins and shape it intentionally?

This chapter is just the beginning of your journey into the hidden power of your mind. As you dive deeper in the upcoming chapters, you'll discover tools and techniques to unlock the incredible potential that lies within you.

Chapter 3

Hunches, Intuition, and the Inner Compass

Have you ever felt an unexplainable urge to take a different route home, only to later discover you avoided a traffic jam? Or sensed that someone was upset before they even spoke? These experiences stem from your intuition; a natural yet often underappreciated faculty of the human mind that operates beneath the surface of conscious awareness.

Intuition is like a silent guide, providing insights without the need for detailed reasoning. It synthesizes vast amounts of data stored in your subconscious, offering immediate clarity in moments of uncertainty. Unlike logical thought, which can be deliberate and slow, intuition arises spontaneously, often as a gut feeling, flash of insight, or quiet inner knowing.

While society tends to prioritize rationality and evidence-based decision-making, intuition serves as an equally vital counterpart. It bridges the gap between logic and emotion, offering a holistic way of understanding the world. By tuning into your intuitive compass, you can make more confident and aligned decisions in every area of life.

But where does this inner knowing come from? To understand, we must dive deeper into the connection between intuition, the subconscious mind, and the universal pool of infinite intelligence.

As we explored in the previous chapter, your subconscious mind is a vast reservoir of stored experiences, beliefs, and emotional patterns. It operates silently, shaping your perceptions and behaviours in profound ways. However, the subconscious does more than just storing personal memories, it also serves as a gateway to intuition.

The subconscious mind processes information far beyond what the conscious mind can handle, sifting through millions of data points to identify patterns, connections, and insights. This is why intuitive hunches often feel like flashes of insight that bypass logical analysis. Your subconscious picks up on subtle cues from your environment, integrates them with your past experiences, and delivers its conclusions as intuitive signals in the form of gut feelings, sudden ideas, or a sense of knowing.

But the subconscious doesn't work in isolation. It has access to a much larger field of intelligence, a universal repository of knowledge often referred to as **infinite intelligence**.

Infinite intelligence is a term used to describe a universal consciousness, a vast interconnected web of energy and knowledge that transcends individual minds. It has been referenced throughout history in spiritual traditions, philosophical teachings, and even modern science. Mystics speak of the "Akashic Records", a metaphysical library containing the collective wisdom of the universe. Similarly, quantum physics suggests that at a fundamental level, everything in the universe is interconnected through fields of energy and information.

This concept implies that every thought, idea, and solution already exists within this infinite pool of intelligence. Intuition, then, acts as a bridge between your individual mind and this collective consciousness, allowing you to access insights and wisdom that are far beyond your immediate understanding.

How the Subconscious Accesses Infinite Intelligence

The subconscious mind acts as a receiver, like a radio antenna tuning into different frequencies. While your conscious mind is preoccupied with day-to-day tasks, your subconscious is constantly scanning and connecting with this larger field of knowledge. When you experience a moment of intuition, it is as if your subconscious has tuned into the right "station" of infinite intelligence and downloaded the information you needed.

This is why intuition often feels effortless and instantaneous. It bypasses the slower, analytical processes of the conscious mind. It's not just limited to your own thoughts and experiences but can tap into the collective wisdom of humanity, and sometimes even beyond.

Consider moments of creative brilliance, such as when a scientist suddenly solves a complex problem or an artist creates a masterpiece seemingly out of thin air. These individuals often describe the experience as though the idea "came to them" rather than being consciously generated. This phenomenon illustrates the power of intuition as a conduit for infinite intelligence.

Another fascinating aspect of intuition is its ability to connect people across time and space.

Have you ever thought of someone, only for them to call or message you moments later? Or felt an inexplicable connection to a stranger? These experiences suggest that our subconscious minds can communicate with one another through a shared energetic field.

This idea aligns with theories of collective consciousness, where all living beings are connected on a subconscious level. Intuition enables us to access this collective wisdom, fostering empathy, understanding, and even telepathic-like connections.

The Science Behind Intuition

Although intuition might feel like magic, it has a solid foundation in neuroscience and psychology. Your brain constantly processes information, much of which never reaches your conscious awareness. This subconscious processing allows your mind to detect patterns, synthesize data, and offer solutions faster than your logical mind can analyze them.

Psychologists Daniel Kahneman and Amos Tversky introduced the **dual-process theory**, which posits that the human brain relies on two systems for decision making:

1. **System 1 (Intuitive Thinking):** Fast, automatic, and subconscious. This system draws on stored knowledge, emotional cues, and past experiences to provide immediate insights.
2. **System 2 (Analytical Thinking):** Slow, deliberate, and conscious. This system relies on logical analysis and deliberate problem-solving.

Kahneman, in his book *Thinking, Fast and Slow*, emphasizes that System 1 often provides reliable judgments, especially in areas where individuals have developed expertise. For instance, a firefighter might instinctively sense when a building is about to collapse, or a doctor might make an accurate diagnosis based on subtle cues they've unconsciously registered.

Research shows that your subconscious processes up to 11 million bits of information per second, compared to the 40-50 bits managed by your conscious mind, as previously stated in chapter 2. This vast reservoir of information forms the foundation of your intuitive abilities.

Neuroscientists have found that the brain is a pattern-detection machine. Studies using functional MRI (fMRI) have shown that the **ventromedial prefrontal cortex (vmPFC)** plays a crucial role in intuitive decision-making. This region integrates emotional and sensory data from past experiences, allowing the brain to detect patterns and make quick judgments without conscious effort.

In one study conducted by Dr. Antonio Damasio, participants were asked to play a card game while their brain activity was monitored. Remarkably, their bodies began to show physiological stress responses (e.g., sweating or increased heart rate) before they consciously recognized which decks were risky. This demonstrated that the subconscious mind processed the patterns and sent intuitive signals well before the conscious mind caught up.

The brain's ability to detect patterns quickly is a survival mechanism, honed over millennia. For instance, our ancestors relied on intuition to sense danger, interpret subtle changes in their environment, and make life-saving decisions. This evolutionary gift remains with us today, helping us navigate modern challenges in relationships, careers, and personal growth.

One key player in intuitive decision-making is the *gut-brain connection.* The enteric nervous system, often referred to as the "second brain," contains millions of neurons in the digestive tract. It communicates with the brain via the vagus nerve, playing a role in those "gut feelings" you experience during pivotal moments.

The Gut-Brain Connection

The phrase "gut feeling" is more than just a metaphor. Your digestive system contains the enteric nervous system, often referred to as the "second brain," which communicates with your central nervous system through the vagus nerve. This connection explains why intuitive insights are frequently accompanied by physical sensations, like a flutter in your stomach or a tightening in your chest.

The enteric nervous system (ENS) located in the gut, is deeply connected to intuitive insights. Research by Dr. Emeran Mayer, author of *The Mind-Gut Connection*, highlights how the **vagus nerve** allows the gut to communicate with the brain, influencing emotional states and decision-making. This connection explains why intuitive insights are often accompanied by visceral sensations like a "gut feeling."

The Heart-Brain Connection

The **HeartMath Institute** has explored the role of the heart in intuitive processing. Their research suggests that the heart generates an electromagnetic field that interacts with the brain and the environment. They found that the heart often responds to future events milliseconds before the brain does, indicating that intuition might involve not only the subconscious mind but also the energetic field surrounding the body.

In high-pressure situations, intuition can be a life-saving tool. A study published in the journal *Psychological Science* examined the decision-making processes of experienced firefighters, surgeons, and military personnel. The researchers found that these individuals relied heavily on their intuition, which allowed them to make rapid and accurate decisions when time was limited. This ability, honed through years of experience, underscores how intuition draws on deeply embedded knowledge and training.

Types of Intuition

1. Emotional Intuition

This form of intuition helps you read and interpret emotional signals, both in yourself and others. It allows you to sense someone's mood, detect unspoken tensions, or predict how a person might react in a given situation. Have you ever sensed someone's mood before they even spoke a word? Emotional intuition helps you navigate social situations, build deeper connections, and understand unspoken dynamics.

2. Pattern Recognition

Your brain is a master at recognizing patterns, even when you're not consciously aware of it. It is highly adept at identifying patterns based on past experiences. For example, a seasoned chess player can anticipate their opponent's moves without deliberate calculation, relying on an intuitive grasp of the game's flow.

This type of intuition is crucial in fields that require quick decision-making, such as medicine, sports, and business.

3. Creative Intuition

Artists, writers, and innovators often experience bursts of inspiration that seem to come out of nowhere. This creative spark is a form of intuition, allowing them to connect seemingly unrelated ideas and produce groundbreaking work.

Creative intuition arises when your mind connects disparate ideas in novel ways. It's what fuels artistic inspiration, innovative problem-solving, and breakthrough discoveries. Many of history's greatest inventions and works of art began as a spark of intuitive genius.

4. Somatic Intuition

Somatic intuition manifests through physical sensations in your body. For instance, you might feel a sense of heaviness when considering a decision that's not aligned with your values or experience a light, expansive feeling when something feels right.

These bodily signals often accompany intuitive insights, offering guidance in decision-making. Learning to interpret these signals can enhance your decision-making process.

The Role of Intuition in Decision-Making

While logic and analysis have their place, over-reliance on them can sometimes lead to paralysis by overthinking. Intuition provides a counterbalance, enabling you to make swift, confident decisions when time is limited or when data is incomplete.

In a world that often demands quick decisions with incomplete information, intuition can be a game-changer. It allows you to cut through complexity and gain clarity, especially in situations where logical analysis falls short.

Many successful leaders, entrepreneurs, and creatives attribute their achievements to trusting their instincts. They understand that intuition isn't a replacement for logic but a complementary tool that provides a broader perspective.

Intuition often reveals opportunities and solutions that might otherwise be overlooked in the quest for logical perfection.

However, it's essential to distinguish genuine intuition from fear-based reactions or wishful thinking. Genuine intuition feels clear, calm, and resolute, while decisions driven by fear or desire often carry a sense of urgency or doubt.

While intuition is powerful, it's essential to balance it with rational analysis. For example, if your intuition suggests pursuing a particular career path, use logic to research its feasibility, weigh potential risks, and plan actionable steps. This balanced approach ensures that your decisions are both inspired and well-informed.

Strengthening Your Intuitive Connection

Just as a muscle grows stronger with regular exercise, your intuitive abilities can be developed and refined with practice. Here are some techniques to deepen your connection to intuition and the infinite intelligence:

1. Practice Mindfulness

Stay present and attuned to your surroundings. Mindfulness sharpens your awareness, helping you notice the subtle signals your intuition provides.

Mindfulness helps quiet the noise of the conscious mind, making it easier to tune into your intuitive insights. Spend a few minutes each day in stillness or meditation, observing your thoughts without judgment.

2. Keep an Intuition Journal

Document moments when you've followed your intuition and note the outcomes. Keeping a journal helps you tune into your inner thoughts and feelings. Write down any hunches, dreams, or intuitive flashes you experience. Over time, you may notice patterns and recurring themes that offer valuable guidance.

3. Pay Attention to Your Body

Learn to interpret your body's signals. Are you feeling tension, lightness, or a sense of warmth when considering a particular decision? These physical cues can provide valuable insight.

4. Ask Open-Ended Questions

When faced with a decision, pose open-ended questions to your subconscious, such as, "What feels right?" or "What's the best course of action?" Then, allow your intuition to provide answers through thoughts, images, or feelings.

5. Engage in Creative Activities

Creativity often taps into your subconscious mind, strengthening your intuitive faculties. Explore activities like painting, journaling, or brainstorming without self-judgment.

6. Pay Attention to Dreams

Your subconscious often communicates through dreams. Keep a dream journal and note any recurring symbols, themes, or feelings that might provide intuitive guidance.

7. Visualization

Spend time visualizing your goals and desired outcomes. Imagine yourself achieving success, happiness, or resolution in a specific situation. This practice not only programs your subconscious but also strengthens your intuitive alignment with your goals.

8. Trust Your Gut

Intuition often speaks through physical sensations like a flutter in your stomach, a sudden sense of calm, or a tingling sensation. Pay attention to these subtle cues and trust your instincts, even if they don't initially make sense.

Your brain is naturally wired to identify patterns and highlight relevant information without conscious effort. This ability amplifies your intuitive sense, helping you notice opportunities and connections that align with your goals and focus. For example, if you're actively seeking a solution to a problem, your subconscious will nudge you toward relevant resources, people, or ideas.

Rather than relying on the mechanics of the RAS, which will be covered in depth in chapter 7, trust that your mind has an innate way of filtering for what's important. By aligning your focus and attention, you'll naturally notice the subtle cues your intuition provides.

When you start trusting and following your intuition, life takes on a new rhythm. Decisions become easier, opportunities seem to appear at the right moment, and challenges feel more manageable. Your inner compass guides you to the people, places, and experiences that align with your highest potential.

By embracing the connection between your subconscious and infinite intelligence, you unlock a source of wisdom that can transform every aspect of your life, from personal relationships to professional endeavors.

Intuition is not a magical gift given to only a few; it's a natural ability that resides within each of us. The key is learning to recognize, trust, and act upon its guidance. As you continue your journey, remember that your inner compass is always pointing you towards growth, fulfillment, and alignment with the greater flow of life.

The next time you feel a hunch or hear that quiet inner voice, pause and listen. It just might be your subconscious tapping into the infinite well of wisdom, offering you the answers you seek.

The adventure of life becomes infinitely richer when you learn to navigate it with the guidance of your intuition. Trust the process, and let your inner compass lead the way.

Developing trust in your intuition takes time and experience. Start by experimenting with small decisions, such as choosing a book to read or a route to take, and observe the results. As your confidence grows, you'll feel more comfortable relying on your intuition for more significant choices.

Intuition is not about rejecting rational thought but about taking-up a deeper, more holistic way of knowing.

Chapter 4

Dreams as Portals - Exploring the Language of the Unconscious

Every night as you sleep, your conscious mind takes a step back, allowing your subconscious to communicate in its unique language - "dreams". Far from being random or meaningless, dreams serve as profound portals to your inner world, offering insights, guidance, and resolutions that often elude your waking mind.

Research in neuroscience and psychology supports the idea that dreams play a crucial role in emotional processing, memory consolidation, and problem-solving. Dr. Rosalind Cartwright, a pioneer in dream research, suggested that dreaming serves as a form of overnight therapy, helping individuals process unresolved emotions and experiences.

By understanding the symbolic language of dreams, you gain access to a wealth of knowledge hidden in your subconscious. These nocturnal messages can illuminate your path, reveal hidden fears, and inspire creative breakthroughs.

Dreams have fascinated humanity for thousands of years. Ancient civilizations saw them as messages from the Gods, while modern science offers a more systematic perspective. Let's examine their primary purposes:

- **Emotional Processing and Healing**

  Dreams play a crucial role in helping us process emotions and manage the psychological challenges of our waking lives. This function is especially pronounced during REM (Rapid Eye Movement) sleep, a phase characterized by vivid and often emotionally charged dreams. During REM sleep, the brain actively revisits and works through complex emotions, transforming raw, overwhelming feelings into more manageable forms.

  How Dreams Process Emotions:

  The brain undergoes a unique state during REM sleep, where activity in the amygdala (the brain's emotional center) remains high, while the prefrontal cortex (responsible for rational thinking and decision-making) is less active. This combination allows the mind to explore and process emotions in a freer, less inhibited way, without the constraints of logical analysis or immediate real world consequences.

  Dreaming provides a "safe space" for emotional processing, enabling the subconscious to work through unresolved feelings, conflicts, and traumatic memories. By simulating emotionally intense scenarios, dreams allow us to face and integrate these experiences, helping to reduce their emotional charge over time.

  The Role of REM Sleep in Emotional Healing:

  A 2017 study led by Dr. Matthew Walker, a neuroscientist at the University of California, Berkeley, offered compelling evidence for the emotional healing power of dreams. The research found that REM sleep helps individuals revisit painful or traumatic experiences in a neurochemical state that lowers emotional intensity. During REM, levels of norepinephrine, a stress related neurotransmitter, drop significantly, allowing the brain to process distressing memories without triggering the same level of emotional reactivity as when we are awake.

This process, described by Dr. Walker as "overnight therapy," highlights how dreams help to desensitize the emotional impact of difficult experiences. For instance, someone who has experienced a traumatic event may initially feel intense fear or anxiety when recalling it. However, after multiple REM cycles, these memories may evoke a more subdued emotional response, enabling the individual to integrate the experience without being overwhelmed.

Research has also shown that dreams are particularly important for people recovering from trauma. Individuals with Post-Traumatic Stress Disorder (PTSD) often experience disrupted REM sleep and recurring nightmares that replay the traumatic event.

The Connection Between Dreams and Emotional Intelligence:

Beyond trauma, dreams play a role in recalibrating everyday emotional states. For example, if you've had a stressful day, your dreams might replay elements of those experiences, helping to diffuse tension and restore emotional equilibrium. Studies suggest that people who experience REM-rich sleep are better able to cope with emotional challenges and exhibit greater emotional resilience.

By processing emotions in dreams, we become more emotionally attuned and adaptive in waking life. This connection may explain why people who pay attention to their dreams often report heightened emotional awareness and improved problem-solving skills in their relationships and personal lives.

- **Problem Solving and Creativity**

Many of history's great innovations were inspired by dreams. For example, Dmitri Mendeleev famously dreamed of the periodic table's structure, and Paul McCartney composed the melody of "Yesterday" in a dream. This phenomenon underscores how dreams can bypass conscious limitations, providing creative solutions to complex problems.

Dreams have long been a wellspring of creativity and innovation, providing solutions to problems and inspiring groundbreaking ideas. The dream state allows the brain to access a unique form of thinking, unencumbered by the constraints of logic, social norms, or linear reasoning. By exploring possibilities beyond the conscious mind's habitual patterns, dreams serve as an invaluable tool for problem-solving and creative breakthroughs.

Dmitri Mendeleev and the Periodic Table:

In 1869, Russian chemist Dmitri Mendeleev was struggling to organize the known elements in a coherent way. After days of frustration, he reportedly had a dream in which the structure of the periodic table appeared to him in a clear and orderly fashion. Upon waking, he wrote down what he saw, laying the foundation for modern chemistry.

Paul McCartney's "Yesterday":

Paul McCartney, a member of The Beatles, famously dreamed the melody of one of the most iconic songs in music history, "Yesterday." He woke up, rushed to his piano, and played the tune exactly as it had appeared in his dream. The song became a global sensation and is considered one of the greatest compositions of all time.

Elias Howe and the Sewing Machine:

Elias Howe, the inventor of the modern sewing machine, was stuck on the problem of where to place the needle's eye. One night, he dreamed of being surrounded by warriors carrying spears with holes at the tips. Upon waking, he realized that the needle's eye could be at its point rather than the other end, leading to his revolutionary invention.

Albert Einstein's Theory of Relativity:

Albert Einstein often credited his dreams with inspiring some of his most profound insights. One notable dream involved him sledding down a mountainside at the speed of light, which contributed to his later development of the theory of relativity.

How Dreams Foster Problem-Solving

Dreams facilitate problem-solving by allowing the brain to process information in a non-linear and imaginative way. This is particularly effective for tackling challenges that seem insurmountable during waking hours.

In the dream state, the conscious mind takes a backseat, allowing the subconscious to explore creative and unconventional solutions. This detachment from logical constraints can reveal possibilities that might otherwise be dismissed as impractical or irrelevant.

During sleep, the brain consolidates memories and reorganizes information, forming new neural connections. This process often leads to insights and fresh perspectives, as the mind integrates disparate pieces of information into coherent patterns.

The subconscious mind operates on a much broader and deeper level than the conscious mind. In dreams, it synthesizes ideas, memories, and emotions, creating a fertile ground for innovative thinking. This is why artists, writers, and scientists frequently report breakthroughs occurring in their dreams.

Dreams act as a mental laboratory where the mind can simulate different scenarios and test creative solutions without real-world consequences. This provides a safe environment for experimentation, encouraging bold and imaginative problem-solving.

The Science Behind Dreams and Creativity

Modern neuroscience offers insights into why dreams are so effective for problem-solving and creativity.

1. **Brain Activity During REM Sleep**

   The **prefrontal cortex**, responsible for critical thinking and self-censorship, becomes less active during REM sleep. At the same time, areas like the **amygdala** and **hippocampus**, which govern emotions and memory, are highly active. This unique brain state allows for free association, emotional insight, and novel connections.

2. **The Default Mode Network (DMN)**

   The DMN, a network of brain regions active during rest and introspection, plays a key role in creative thought. During dreams, the DMN facilitates spontaneous and imaginative thinking, helping the brain generate innovative ideas and solutions.

3. **The Role of Neurotransmitters**

   REM sleep involves a decrease in **serotonin** and **norepinephrine**, which are associated with focused attention, and an increase in **acetylcholine**, which promotes vivid imagery and emotional intensity. This neurochemical environment enhances the brain's ability to explore abstract ideas and creative solutions.

Engaging Your Creative Faculty Through Dreams

By paying attention to your dreams and intentionally engaging with their messages, you can tap into a powerful source of creativity and insight. Dreams offer a window into the subconscious, where the boundaries of logic dissolve, and the mind can freely explore new ideas. Whether you're seeking to solve a complex problem, overcome a creative block, or innovate in your field, your dreams can serve as a guiding light, leading you to discoveries beyond your conscious imagination.

Dreams provide an unparalleled opportunity to access the boundless potential of the subconscious mind. Unlike the conscious state, where logic and structure often confine our thinking, dreams operate in a realm free of constraints, allowing ideas to flow and merge in unexpected ways. This makes dreams a powerful tool for creativity, offering fresh perspectives and solutions that may elude the conscious mind. By paying attention to your dreams and actively engaging with their symbols, narratives, and emotions, you open a gateway to a reservoir of untapped inspiration and insight.

Creative breakthroughs often occur when the conscious mind is at rest, and dreams can play a pivotal role in this process. The surreal landscapes and symbolic imagery of dreams encourage lateral thinking, helping individuals explore unconventional paths and make connections that might seem illogical in waking life. This is particularly useful for those facing creative blocks, as dreams can bypass mental barriers and reveal innovative solutions. For example, Salvador Dalí, the renowned surrealist painter, drew inspiration from his dreams to create some of his most iconic works. Similarly, modern professionals- from artists and writers to scientists and entrepreneurs can benefit from embracing their dreams as a source of guidance and inspiration, leading to breakthroughs in their respective fields.

To fully harness the creative potential of dreams, it is important to cultivate an intentional practice of dream engagement. This can include keeping a dream journal to record and reflect on recurring themes or vivid imagery, meditating on dream messages for deeper understanding, or practicing dream incubation, where one sets an intention before sleep to seek insight on a specific question or challenge. By integrating these practices into your routine, you can build a deeper connection with your subconscious, enhancing your ability to solve problems, innovate, and express yourself creatively. Ultimately, engaging with your dreams not only enriches your inner world but also empowers your waking life, enabling you to approach challenges and opportunities with a fresh, imaginative perspective.

- **Symbolic Communication**

  Dreams often communicate in the language of symbols, using imagery and scenarios that may seem strange or disconnected at first glance. Unlike the straightforward language of the waking mind, the dream world relies on metaphor and symbolism to convey its messages. This symbolic nature allows dreams to bypass the constraints of logical thought, offering insights from the deeper layers of the psyche.

  Renowned psychologist Carl Jung devoted much of his work to understanding this symbolic communication. He believed that dreams serve as a bridge between the conscious and unconscious mind, helping individuals integrate hidden aspects of themselves. At the heart of Jung's theory is the concept of **archetypes**: universal, recurring symbols that emerge across cultures and time. These archetypes, such as the Hero, the Shadow, or the Wise Old Man, represent fundamental aspects of the human experience.

  For example, dreaming of a journey might symbolize personal growth, while encountering a shadowy figure could represent repressed fears or desires. A dream of flying might signify freedom and a broader perspective, whereas being chased could reflect unresolved anxieties or challenges. These symbols aren't random; they offer meaningful insights tailored to the dreamer's current life circumstances and inner struggles.

Jung proposed that dreams perform a vital role in the process of **individuation** - the journey towards self-awareness and wholeness. By understanding and integrating the messages contained in dream symbols, individuals can achieve greater harmony between their conscious intentions and unconscious motivations.

Research Supporting Symbolic Communication

Modern research in the field of dream analysis has provided support for the idea that dreams use symbols to convey meaning. Studies have shown that dreams often reflect a person's waking concerns, but they do so in a metaphorical way. For instance, one study published in the *Journal of Personality and Social Psychology* found that people dreaming about stressful situations frequently experience symbolic representations of those stressors, rather than literal recreations.

Neuroimaging research further supports the symbolic nature of dreams. Brain scans during REM sleep show heightened activity in areas responsible for emotion and memory, such as the amygdala and hippocampus, while regions linked to rational thinking, like the prefrontal cortex, are less active. This shift may explain why dreams favour symbolic and emotional content over logical, linear narratives.

Interpreting Dream Symbols

Interpreting dream symbols requires personal reflection, as their meanings can vary depending on the dreamer's experiences, beliefs, and cultural background. For example, water might symbolize purification and renewal for one person but evoke feelings of fear or drowning for another. To decode these symbols, Jung encouraged exploring associations and emotions linked to the dream imagery.

Dream journals can be a valuable tool in this process. By recording and analyzing dreams over time, patterns and recurring symbols may emerge, offering deeper insights into the dreamer's subconscious mind.

Cultural Perspectives on Dream Symbols

Across different cultures, dreams and their symbols have been interpreted in diverse ways. In ancient Egyptian culture, dreams were seen as divine messages, and priests specialized in dream interpretation. In Native American traditions, dreams are often viewed as spiritual journeys or visions that provide guidance and healing.

Despite cultural differences, common symbols such as journeys, animals, and natural elements appear universally. This shared dream imagery supports Jung's idea of a **collective unconscious**, a shared reservoir of archetypal symbols and themes that all humans inherit.

- **Memory Consolidation**
  Dreams play a crucial role in the brain's ability to process, store, and organize memories. Neuroscientists have found that sleep, particularly the REM and deep sleep stages, is essential for memory consolidation. It's the process by which short-term memories are transformed into long-term, stable ones. Dreams are an integral part of this process, offering a unique environment for the brain to integrate new information, strengthen neural pathways, and enhance cognitive functions like learning and problem-solving.
  Memory consolidation occurs in two main stages of sleep:

1. **Slow-Wave Sleep (SWS)**
   During SWS, the brain replays recent experiences, transferring information from the **hippocampus** (short-term memory storage) to the **neocortex**, where long-term memories are stored. This replay process solidifies factual

and declarative memories, such as names, dates, and concepts.

2. **REM Sleep**
   REM sleep is associated with the consolidation of emotional and procedural memories, such as learning a new skill or navigating social interactions. Dreams during this stage often weave together fragments of recent experiences, older memories, and symbolic imagery, helping the brain create meaningful connections between disparate pieces of information.

The Role of Dreams in Memory Consolidation:

1. Integrating New Knowledge
   Dreams allow the brain to connect newly acquired information with existing knowledge. This integration helps in developing a deeper understanding of complex concepts and facilitates creative problem-solving.
2. Emotional Memory Processing
   Emotionally charged memories are often prioritized for consolidation. Dreams provide a safe space for the brain to process and resolve emotional experiences, reducing the intensity of negative emotions while retaining the core lessons or insights.
3. Strengthening Neural Pathways
   During sleep, synaptic connections related to newly learned information are strengthened, while irrelevant or redundant information is pruned. This selective process ensures that important memories are retained and easily accessible.
4. Rehearsal and Simulation
   Dreams often simulate real-life scenarios, providing a form of mental rehearsal. For instance, dreaming about giving a presentation or practicing a skill can improve performance by reinforcing the neural circuits involved.

The Sleep and Learning Study (2007):
A study by Robert Stickgold at Harvard Medical School demonstrated that participants who took a nap after learning a task performed significantly better than those who remained awake. Those who experienced REM sleep, in particular, showed the greatest improvement, highlighting the role of dreams in consolidating learning and enhancing performance.

Walker's Memory Experiments (2011):
Neuroscientist Matthew Walker conducted experiments showing that sleep, especially the REM stage, helps integrate new experiences into existing memory networks. His research found that participants who dreamed about a task they were learning (e.g., navigating a maze) performed better than those who did not dream about it.

Emotional Memory Study (2013):
A study published in Current Biology found that REM sleep plays a critical role in processing emotional memories. Participants who experienced REM sleep after viewing emotionally charged images showed reduced emotional reactivity to the images upon waking, demonstrating how dreams help in managing and retaining emotional content.

Types of Memories Consolidated During Sleep:

1. Declarative Memory
   Facts, knowledge, and experiences are consolidated during SWS and REM sleep. For example, studying for an exam before sleeping can enhance recall due to memory integration during dreams.

2. Procedural Memory
   Skills like playing an instrument, typing, or riding a bike are solidified during REM sleep. Dreaming about these activities can enhance muscle memory and coordination.

3. Emotional Memory
   Dreams process emotionally significant events, helping to regulate mood and reduce the impact of trauma while preserving key lessons.

4. Spatial Memory
   Dreams also aid in consolidating spatial memories, such as navigating a new city or remembering the layout of a building.

The Brain's Key Players in Memory Consolidation:

Hippocampus
The hippocampus acts as a temporary storage site for new information. During sleep, it communicates with the neocortex to transfer and integrate memories.

Neocortex
The neocortex is where long-term memories are stored. Dreams play a role in strengthening connections within this region, allowing memories to become more permanent.

Amygdala
The amygdala processes emotions and plays a critical role in consolidating emotionally charged memories. Its heightened activity during REM sleep explains why dreams often have strong emotional content.

Memory consolidation is one of the most important functions of sleep and dreams. By organizing and integrating new information, dreams help the brain optimize learning, problem-solving, and emotional regulation. Far from being mere nighttime entertainment, dreams are essential for cognitive and emotional well-being, providing insights and connections that shape our waking lives. Incorporating the power of dreams can unlock new levels of understanding and creativity, helping us retain what matters most and letting go of the rest.

Types of Dreams

Dreams manifest in various forms, each offering unique insights:

1. **Symbolic Dreams**
   The most common type, these dreams rely on metaphors and symbols to communicate. For example, dreaming of climbing a mountain might symbolize striving towards a goal or overcoming an obstacle.
2. **Lucid Dreams**
   Lucid dreaming occurs when you become aware that you're dreaming and can consciously interact with the dream. A 2009 study by Ursula Voss and colleagues found that lucid dreaming activates parts of the prefrontal cortex, offering a rare blend of conscious and subconscious experience.
3. **Prophetic Dreams**
   Also known as precognitive dreams, these seem to predict future events. While science remains cautious about labeling these experiences as truly prophetic, they may reflect the subconscious mind's ability to detect patterns and foresee potential outcomes.
4. **Recurring Dreams**
   Recurring dreams highlight unresolved issues or repetitive life themes. They often signify areas where personal growth or healing is needed.

5. **Nightmares**
   Nightmares serve as warnings or emotional catharsis, revealing fears and anxieties that require conscious attention.

Interpreting dreams requires sensitivity to their symbolic and emotional content. While dream dictionaries can offer general guidance, personal associations are crucial for meaningful interpretation.

For instance:

- Water: Represents emotions. Calm water might signify tranquility, while turbulent water reflects inner conflict.
- Flying: Suggests freedom or rising above challenges.
- Being Chased: Indicates avoidance of a problem or fear.
- Doors or Pathways: Symbolize transitions or new opportunities.

To decode your dreams:

1. Record Them Immediately: Keep a dream journal to capture details before they fade.
2. Analyze Emotional Tone: Was the dream joyful, frightening, or neutral?
3. Identify Symbols and Patterns: Reflect on how they relate to your waking life.

Modern research has demystified many aspects of dreaming, showing its crucial role in cognitive and emotional functioning.

- **REM Sleep and Memory:** During REM sleep, the brain processes emotional memories and integrates new information. A 2018 study by the Sleep Research Society found that REM sleep enhances creative problem-solving by strengthening weak associations in the brain.
- **Theta Brainwaves:** Dreams are associated with theta brainwaves, which facilitate intuitive insights and deep emotional processing.

Neuroscientist Jay Giedd suggests that these waves create an optimal state for the subconscious to process unresolved issues and generate creative ideas.

The Connection Between Dreams and Infinite Intelligence

Dreams serve as more than just reflections of personal experiences; they are a gateway to the universal pool of infinite intelligence. This vast field of interconnected knowledge holds insights, ideas, and solutions that transcend your conscious understanding. When you dream, your subconscious mind taps into this collective reservoir, bringing back symbols, visions, and intuitive flashes that often contain profound meaning.

Carl Jung's concept of the collective unconscious aligns with this idea, proposing that dreams draw on archetypes - universal symbols and patterns shared across humanity. These archetypes, such as the hero, the shadow, or the wise old man, carry timeless lessons and guidance. For example, dreaming of a journey or a staircase may symbolize your personal growth or spiritual ascent, connecting your individual experience to a larger, universal story. In this way, dreams become a bridge between your inner psyche and the greater intelligence of the cosmos, offering wisdom that can guide your decisions, spark your creativity, and illuminate your life's path.

Your dreams are more than fleeting images; they are powerful tools for personal evolution and self-discovery. By paying attention to your dreams, you unlock a wealth of insights about your thoughts, emotions, and deeper desires. Dreams often reveal hidden aspects of yourself- fears you've suppressed, aspirations you've overlooked, or unresolved conflicts that need your attention. By interpreting these messages, you gain clarity and direction in your waking life.

Beyond self-awareness, dreams connect you to a higher wisdom that can act as a guiding force. They can offer solutions to problems, inspire creative breakthroughs, and even reveal glimpses of future possibilities. For instance, many people have reported receiving vivid dream messages that shaped their careers, relationships, or spiritual journeys. When you learn to trust the subtle guidance of your subconscious, your dreams become catalysts for growth, helping you align with your true purpose and navigate life's challenges with greater confidence and ease.

Chapter 5

Reprogramming Your Inner World

When we stand in front of a mirror and smile, the reflection smiles back. When we frown, the reflection frowns too. It doesn't act independently, it simply reflects what it sees. Life works in a similar way. Your external experiences: your relationships, career, health, and even the opportunities that come your way are mirrors of your inner world, shaped by your thoughts, beliefs, and emotions.

Your subconscious mind acts like the programming behind the scenes. It runs quietly in the background, shaping how you see and interpret the world. If your subconscious beliefs are rooted in fear, scarcity, or self-doubt, your outer reality will reflect these limitations. Conversely, if your inner world is grounded in confidence, abundance, and purpose, life tends to mirror those positive qualities back to you.

Think of it this way: reprogramming your inner world is like adjusting a camera lens. A blurry or smudged lens distorts the view, making everything seem unclear or overwhelming. But when you clean and focus the lens, the world comes into sharp clarity, and previously hidden details become visible. Similarly, when you align your inner world with empowering beliefs and emotions, you start to see life's opportunities, solutions, and beauty more clearly.

Why Does This Matter?

Most people spend their lives trying to change external circumstances - working harder for success, seeking validation in relationships, or chasing happiness through material possessions. While these pursuits might offer temporary satisfaction, they don't address the root cause of dissatisfaction: the inner world.

For example: someone who repeatedly struggles with money, no matter how much they earn. They might try budgeting or taking on extra work, but their financial reality remains a challenge. Often, the real issue lies in subconscious beliefs like "I'm not good with money" or "I don't deserve wealth." These beliefs act as invisible barriers, preventing financial progress. By reprogramming these limiting beliefs, people can break free from old patterns and experience true abundance.

Your inner world determines how you perceive challenges and opportunities. Two people might face the same situation; a job loss, for instance - but their internal programming will shape their responses. One person might spiral into despair, believing, "I'm a failure; I'll never find another job." Another might see it as an opportunity, thinking, "This is my chance to find something I truly love." The difference lies in their subconscious beliefs, not the external event.

Reprogramming your inner world allows you to shift from a mindset of limitation to one of possibility. When you let go of old fears and doubts, you open the door to new experiences and a deeper sense of fulfillment. It's not about ignoring challenges but approaching them with a sense of empowerment and clarity.

Think about a garden. If the soil is rocky, full of weeds, or lacks nutrients, no matter how many seeds you plant, the garden won't flourish. The plants might grow weakly or not grow at all. But when you take the time to nurture the soil, removing the rocks, pulling the weeds, and enriching it with nutrients, those same seeds can thrive and produce a beautiful, bountiful garden.

Your subconscious mind is exactly like that soil. If it's filled with limiting beliefs, self-doubt, or unresolved emotional baggage, it's difficult for the seeds of your goals and dreams to grow. But by nurturing and reprogramming your inner world, you create fertile ground for those dreams to flourish.

In essence, the power to change your life starts from within. Just as a mirror reflects what's before it, your external reality reflects the state of your inner world. When you shift your internal programming, you'll notice a profound transformation in how you experience the world around you. You'll start seeing not just obstacles, but opportunities; not just scarcity, but abundance; not just struggles, but pathways to growth.

From the moment we are born, our minds absorb information like a sponge. As children, we form beliefs based on our environment, family dynamics, and early experiences. These beliefs, often operating below our conscious awareness, become mental programs that dictate how we interpret and respond to life. They can empower us, driving us towards success, or limit us, keeping us stuck in cycles of fear and self-doubt.

Imagine your mind as a computer, and your subconscious beliefs as the software running it. From the moment you're born, your brain begins downloading "programs" based on your environment, family dynamics, and early experiences. These mental programs formed during your most impressionable years shape how you see yourself and the world around you. Over time, they create an invisible blueprint that guides your decisions, influences your behaviour, and even determines your emotional responses.

For instance, a child raised in an environment where success is celebrated and mistakes are seen as learning opportunities might develop a mental program of confidence and resilience. They'll likely approach challenges with a "can-do" attitude, seeing setbacks as stepping stones. On the other hand, a child who grows up in a critical or fear-based environment might internalize beliefs like "I'm not good enough" or "The world is a dangerous place," leading to patterns of self-doubt, hesitation, or avoidance in adulthood.

These mental programs, often running silently in the background, influence every facet of your life; your relationships, career choices, financial habits, and even your physical health. For example, if you carry a belief that "relationships always end in heartbreak," you might unconsciously sabotage connections or shy away from intimacy altogether. Similarly, a mental program like "money is the root of all evil" could prevent you from fully embracing financial opportunities, even if they're within reach.

The key to understanding the power of mental programming lies in its subtlety. Many of these beliefs were formed so early in life that they feel like absolute truths rather than learned perspectives. You may not even realize how much they dictate your thoughts and actions. Recognizing that these scripts are not set in stone is the first step towards transformation.

But, just as software can be updated, so can your mental programs. The brain is remarkably adaptable, thanks to a concept known as **neuroplasticity** (the brain's ability to reorganize itself by forming new neural connections). This means that with conscious effort, you can identify and replace outdated, limiting beliefs with empowering ones. We will discuss this topic in a lot more depth in chapter 8.

Let us take an example to understand this better: let's say you've always believed, "I'm terrible at public speaking." This belief likely stems from a past experience where you felt embarrassed or judged while speaking in front of others. By revisiting and reframing that memory, you can create a new narrative: "I've learned from my past, and I'm growing more confident every time I speak." Over time, with practice and positive reinforcement, this new belief will take root, replacing the old script.

Think of your mental programming like a GPS in your car. If the GPS is set to direct you to a specific location, let's say a town you visited as a child, it will guide you there even if you're trying to head somewhere new. To reach your desired destination, you need to update the GPS with new coordinates. Similarly, to achieve your goals and live a more fulfilling life, you must reprogram your mental blueprint with beliefs that align with where you want to go, not where you've been.

The first step in rewriting your mental blueprint is awareness. Start by observing recurring patterns in your life, especially in areas where you feel stuck or unfulfilled. Ask yourself:

- What beliefs might be driving these patterns?
- Where did these beliefs come from?
- Are they serving me, or are they holding me back?

Once you identify, you can begin the process of consciously choosing new, empowering beliefs to replace them.

The Science of Rewiring the Brain

Thanks to advances in neuroscience, we now know that the brain is not a static organ. Neuroplasticity, the brain's ability to form and reorganize neural connections, means that old thought patterns can be replaced with new, empowering ones. Dr. Joe Dispenza, a leading expert in this field, describes how intentional practice can rewire the brain: "When you break the habit of being yourself, and truly change your mind, your life will change."

This plasticity is a hopeful reminder that no matter how deeply ingrained your current beliefs may be, they are not permanent. Like a well-trodden path in a forest, old neural connections may take time to fade, but with consistent effort, new pathways can emerge, leading you to a brighter reality.

The Role of Beliefs and Self-Talk

Beliefs act as the foundation of your subconscious programming. If you hold the belief that success is only for the privileged, your actions will reflect that limitation. On the other hand, a belief in your limitless potential fuels confidence and action towards your goals. Self-talk, the internal dialogue you engage in daily, plays a critical role in reinforcing these beliefs.

Most of us have faced or seen someone facing the following situation in life- if a friend or a family member constantly criticizes or doubts you, it erodes your self-esteem. Now imagine how much damage negative self-talk can cause over time. Once we start thinking and speaking of success, new possibilities and positive things in life, life slowly starts to turn that way.

One of the most powerful ways to reprogram your subconscious is through affirmations and visualization. Repeating positive statements like "I am capable and worthy" helps overwrite negative mental scripts. When paired with vivid mental imagery, your subconscious begins to accept these affirmations as reality. You will get a clear blueprint of these techniques in the upcoming chapters.

Meditation is another tool that allows you to access a state of deep relaxation, where the conscious mind quiets, and the subconscious becomes more receptive. Another effective technique is Emotional Freedom Techniques (EFT), or tapping, which combines physical stimulation of specific acupressure points with affirmations to release emotional blocks.

Even something as simple as practicing gratitude can have a profound impact. By focusing on what you're thankful for, you train your brain to look for positivity, gradually shifting your mental programming toward abundance.

When you clear limiting beliefs, you naturally align with the universal pool of infinite intelligence. It's a limitless source of wisdom, creativity, and inspiration. Think of this as tuning into a radio frequency that broadcasts solutions and ideas beyond your conscious grasp. As you align with this frequency, synchronicities, insights, and creative breakthroughs become more common, guiding you towards your highest potential.

Overcoming Resistance to Change

Changing your mental programming isn't always easy. Resistance often comes in the form of fear, doubt, or old habits resurfacing. This is your subconscious mind trying to maintain its status quo. Acknowledge this resistance without judgment and remind yourself why reprogramming is essential for your growth.

Remember, small steps lead to big changes. Celebrate each moment of progress, no matter how minor it seems. Over time, persistence will transform even the most stubborn mental patterns.

Countless individuals have rewritten their mental scripts and achieved remarkable success. Consider Oprah Winfrey, who overcame a challenging upbringing by reprogramming her beliefs about self-worth and possibility. Her journey reminds us that the stories we tell ourselves shape our reality.

Remember that you are both- the author and the architect of your life. Reprogramming your inner world allows you to create a reality that aligns with your dreams and aspirations.

By reprogramming your subconscious, you gain the power to shape your life intentionally. No longer at the mercy of old mental scripts, you can achieve your true potential and live with greater clarity, purpose, and joy. The process requires dedication, but the rewards are transformative.

Your inner world is the foundation of everything you experience. Trust in the process, and always remember that "**the power to change your life lies within you**".

Chapter 6

How the Subconscious Shapes Reality

Have you heard of the mirror effect?

Since ages, we have heard our parents, grand-parents and all the elders saying "Speak positive, stay positive", "don't speak negatively, or negative things may happen". Normally, as most children do, we ignore the statement, thinking that it's all crap. How can anything happen, based on what I speak?

The truth is, those statements are actually factually correct! Yes, even though our parents or elders may or may not know the science or working behind it, but that actually stands true.

Let's take an example: if you subconsciously believe that success is only attainable through struggle, you may find yourself constantly facing obstacles, even when opportunities arise. Conversely, if your subconscious holds the belief that you are worthy of love and abundance, you'll naturally gravitate towards experiences and people that affirm those beliefs.

But the question is, how does it actually happen?

Your subconscious doesn't just create your reality, it shapes how you perceive it. Let's say two people walk into the same room filled with strangers. One person, who subconsciously believes they're socially awkward, may feel judged and out of place. Meanwhile, another individual, confident in his social abilities, might perceive the same group as friendly and welcoming. The external environment hasn't changed, but their inner programming filters their perception, creating vastly different experiences.

This filtering process is why two people can face identical circumstances but react in entirely different ways. Your subconscious interprets events based on the mental programs you've accumulated over time, shaping your emotional responses and the actions you take.

The question from the beginning of this chapter is still unanswered? Don't worry, you'll understand everything before completing this chapter.

Where Science Meets Metaphysics (The Mechanics of Reality Creation)

The connection between your subconscious and reality isn't just spiritual philosophy, it's supported by science. Your thoughts, beliefs, and emotional patterns quietly influence how you behave, what you notice, and even what you attract in life. When those internal settings go unexamined, you might not even realize how much they're steering your life.

Let's break this down with an example. Imagine preparing for a job interview. One person walks in with a subtle inner voice saying, *"I'm not qualified enough for this."* Their posture shrinks a little, their voice wavers, and they read every raised eyebrow or scribbled note as a sign of rejection. Meanwhile, another person enters with the belief, *"I have value to offer."* They carry themselves with calm confidence, speak with ease, and interpret those same scribbles and silences as part of the process, not judgment.

It's the same room, same interviewers but two entirely different experiences. That difference wasn't created by the external situation; it was actually shaped by what each person brought in internally.

This is where science and metaphysics meet. Research in psychology shows that your brain naturally looks for information that confirms your existing beliefs; a concept known as **confirmation bias**. So, if your subconscious believes that you're not worthy, your brain will actually seek out and highlight experiences that support that story, while ignoring or dismissing evidence to the contrary. The opposite is true as well. As your beliefs start to change, so does the way you see the world. And without even trying, you start showing up differently and making choices that lead to better results.

Neuroscientists have discovered that your brain rewires itself based on repeated thought patterns and experiences. The more you repeat a thought or belief, the more your mind starts to treat it as truth; and soon, your choices and actions start lining up with that version of reality, often without you even noticing.

For example, if you repeatedly visualize achieving a goal, your brain starts forming neural connections that make this outcome feel familiar and attainable. Over time, you unconsciously align your actions and decisions with this vision, increasing the likelihood of its manifestation.

This ties into what many know as the **law of attraction**: the idea that your thoughts and emotions emit energy that attracts similar frequencies. A kind of energetic frequency that draws in experiences to match. While this sounds metaphysical (and it is), even physics has something to say about it. In quantum theory, particles exist in a state of probability until they are observed. The mere act of observation or focused attention has the power to influence outcomes. In other words, consciousness affects reality at a fundamental level.

So, when you visualize your goals with emotion and clarity, you're not just daydreaming, you're reinforcing those possibilities both in your brain and, potentially, in the energetic fabric of reality itself. Over time, your actions, focus, and emotional alignment begin pulling those imagined outcomes into your lived experience.

You become someone who naturally moves towards that future because, deep down, your subconscious already believes it's possible.

Have you ever expected something to go wrong, and it did? Or felt certain you'd succeed, and everything seemed to fall into place? These are examples of self-fulfilling prophecies, where your subconscious beliefs directly influence your behaviour and outcomes.

That's not just coincidence or luck. It's what psychologists call a **self-fulfilling prophecy**, and it has everything to do with the beliefs you carry in your subconscious mind.

Your subconscious beliefs influence how you carry yourself, the decisions you make, and even how you interpret what's happening around you. These beliefs, whether empowering or limiting, subtly shape your behaviour and that behaviour, in turn, shapes your outcomes.

Let's break it down.

Suppose you believe that no one will ever truly appreciate your work. Without realizing it, you might downplay your efforts, avoid sharing your ideas, or miss opportunities for recognition. The world then mirrors this belief, reinforcing the idea that your contributions go unnoticed.

Let's say you carry the belief that you're "not smart enough" or that people won't take you seriously. Even if it's buried deep in your subconscious, it still shows up. Maybe you hesitate to speak up in meetings, or you avoid taking on challenges because you're afraid of failure. Without meaning to, you send signals through your body language, tone, and actions that confirm the belief you already hold. Others pick up on that energy, and sure enough, you're overlooked or dismissed… again. And so, the belief becomes your reality.

It's not that the world is against you, it's that your own inner self writing how you show up in the world.

Now, consider the opposite. Imagine someone who truly believes, deep down, that they are capable and worthy of success.

That person is likely to take more initiative, handle rejection without spiralling, and keep showing up with energy and optimism. As a result, they're seen as confident, capable, and even inspiring. They attract more opportunities because they *believe* they deserve them and their actions reflect that.

It's not magic. It's psychology. Confidence signals competence. Persistence leads to progress. People respond to the energy you bring and that energy comes from the beliefs you hold inside.

Once you begin to recognize these patterns in your own life, you gain the power to shift them. Start paying attention to the story you tell yourself. Especially in moments of doubt, fear, or hesitation. Is that story helping you grow, or holding you back?

This doesn't mean pretending everything is perfect or never feeling insecure. It means choosing to challenge the automatic thoughts and beliefs that no longer serve you. You don't have to accept them as truth just because they've been around for a long time.

The Role of Emotions in Manifestation

Your emotions are not just fleeting feelings, they're signals; like a radio transmitter, constantly broadcasting the "channel" your subconscious is tuned into. They act like a bridge between what you believe deep down and what you experience in the outer world.

When you're genuinely joyful, grateful, or full of love, you're not just "in a good mood", you're sending out signals that say, "*This is what I'm ready for, this is what I expect more of*". Life tends to respond in kind, showing up with more moments, people, and opportunities that match those feelings. That's why sometimes good days snowball. Your inner state sets a tone that the outer world picks up on.

On the other hand, emotions like fear, resentment, or self-doubt aren't "bad" in a moral sense, but they do anchor you to the beliefs that triggered them. If you feel unworthy, you might hesitate to ask for a raise, keep quiet in meetings, or shy away from new relationships. These emotions quietly instruct your subconscious to scan for proof that you're right, so you end up seeing more situations that confirm your fears.

Emotions are not fixed. You can shift them, and by doing so, you shift the signals your subconscious is sending. That doesn't mean ignoring pain or pretending to be happy, it means learning to acknowledge your feelings, understand where they're coming from, and then gently choose a more empowering state when you're ready.

For example, imagine you're about to give a big presentation. If you focus on how nervous you are, your body might tighten up, your voice might tremble, and your mind will scramble for words. But if you shift into a state of excitement, reminding yourself this is a chance to share something valuable, you'll naturally stand taller, speak more clearly, and engage your audience. Same event, completely different outcome, simply because of the emotional "frequency" you chose to broadcast.

In short, your emotions are both a reflection of your inner world and the steering wheel for where your life is headed. Learn to steer with intention, and you can turn almost any situation into an opportunity for growth and alignment.

The Placebo Effect (Proof of Mind Over Matter)

One of the most compelling scientific examples of how the subconscious shapes reality is the placebo effect. In clinical studies, patients given a sugar pill believing it to be medicine often experience real improvements in their condition. Their subconscious belief in the treatment's efficacy triggers physiological changes, such as reduced pain or improved immunity.

This phenomenon illustrates the immense power of belief. If a mere thought can influence your body's healing processes, imagine the impact of reprogramming your subconscious to support your goals, health, and well-being.

What's happening here isn't magic. It's the subconscious at work. When someone truly believes they're being treated, their brain and body respond as if that's the truth. Hormones shift, immune responses strengthen, and neural pathways signal the body to heal. It's the mind giving the body a green light, saying "*You're on the road to recovery now*".

One famous example comes from a 1955 study by Dr. Henry Beecher, who noticed that soldiers in World War II often recovered from injuries faster than expected, even when given only saline injections instead of morphine. Their belief in the treatment and the trust they had in the medical staff was enough to trigger the body's natural pain-relieving mechanisms.

And it's not limited to physical healing. The placebo effect shows up in mental and emotional well-being too. People who believe they're using a "mood-boosting" pill often report feeling happier, even if it's chemically inert. Their subconscious expectation sets in motion a cascade of changes in brain chemistry and behaviour that make the feeling real.

Now, imagine applying this same principle to other areas of life like your career, your relationships, your personal growth. If the belief in a simple sugar pill can lead to measurable physical recovery, what could happen if you trained your subconscious to believe in your own capabilities, worthiness, and potential? The placebo effect is essentially a glimpse into the raw power of the mind and a reminder that much of what we experience begins with what we expect.

The lesson here is clear, your subconscious doesn't just passively store information, it takes your beliefs as instructions and works tirelessly to bring them to life. Feed it the right instructions, and you might be amazed at how reality starts to shift in your favour.

One of the most famous stories of turning belief into reality comes from actor Jim Carrey. In the early 1990s, long before he was a household name, Carrey was struggling to make ends meet. But instead of letting his circumstances define him, he decided to define his circumstances. He took a blank cheque, wrote it out to himself for **$10 million** with the note "for acting services rendered," and dated it exactly five years into the future. Then he slipped it into his wallet.

It wasn't just a wish, it became a daily, tangible reminder of his goal. Every time he saw that check, it reinforced the idea in his subconscious that he was *already* the kind of actor who commanded that fee. That belief didn't just sit there; it began shaping his choices. He went to auditions with more confidence, approached opportunities with a sense of inevitability, and refused to settle for roles that didn't align with his vision.

Five years later, almost to the date he landed his breakout role in *Dumb and Dumber*, which paid him the exact $10 million he had written down years before.

The real power of this story isn't about luck or coincidence. It's about the way our subconscious works when it's given a clear, consistent message. Carrey's check wasn't magic, it was a tool to repeatedly tell his mind, *This is who I am becoming.* And when your subconscious accepts something as true, it begins nudging you often in subtle, invisible ways towards actions and opportunities that make that truth real.

In a way, Carrey was "programming" himself every time he opened his wallet. And over time, that internal programming became an external reality.

To shape your reality intentionally, it's essential to align your subconscious beliefs with your conscious desires. Start by identifying any conflicting inner narratives. For example, you might consciously desire financial freedom but subconsciously believe that wealth is corrupting or unattainable.

Over time, this alignment creates a seamless flow between your internal world and external experiences.

Shaping your reality isn't just about having big dreams, it's about making sure your subconscious isn't quietly sabotaging those dreams behind the scenes. Think of it like rowing a boat. If your conscious mind is rowing forward but your subconscious is rowing in the opposite direction, you'll stay stuck in the same spot, no matter how hard you paddle.

This is why alignment between your inner and outer worlds is so important. Your conscious desires set the destination, but your subconscious beliefs control the engine. If those beliefs are in conflict, say you consciously want financial freedom but deep down believe "money is hard to come by" or "wealth changes people for the worse", you'll unintentionally make choices that keep you from reaching your goal.

Alignment begins with awareness. Pay attention to your automatic thoughts and emotional reactions. Do you feel uncomfortable when you think about having more money? Do you instinctively distrust people who are successful? These subtle cues reveal the stories your subconscious is telling.

Once you spot these conflicting narratives, you can start to reframe them. This isn't about forcing yourself to think positive all the time, it's about gently introducing new, empowering beliefs that your subconscious can accept. Maybe you start telling yourself, "Money is simply a tool, and in my hands, it can create good." Or, "Success doesn't have to mean sacrifice, it can mean freedom and contribution."

Over time, as these new beliefs take root, you'll notice that your actions, decisions, and even the opportunities you attract begin to shift. That's when the inner and outer worlds start working together, and life begins to flow instead of feeling like an uphill climb.

Trust the process, and remember - "the life you desire is already within you".

Chapter 7

The Reticular Activating System and Perception

Have you ever bought a new car and then almost overnight started spotting that same model everywhere? Or maybe you learned a new word and suddenly it seemed to pop up in conversations, news articles, even on billboards? It feels almost spooky, but it's not magic. It's your brain's Reticular Activating System (RAS) quietly doing its job.

The RAS is a bundle of nerve fibers tucked into your brainstem. Think of it as your mind's personal filter or gatekeeper. Every single second, your senses bombard your brain with an overwhelming amount of information: sights, sounds, smells, textures, movements. Scientists estimate it's in the millions of bits per second. But you only become *consciously* aware of a tiny sliver of that input; around forty bits at most. Without some sort of filter, you'd be drowning in sensory overload every moment of the day.

This filter is incredibly intelligent. It doesn't just block things out randomly, it chooses what gets through based on what your brain has tagged as "important." And that "importance" isn't necessarily logical; it comes from your goals, fears, desires, and deeply held beliefs. If you're nervous about making a presentation, your RAS will zoom in on every yawn or glance at a watch, as if your audience is bored. If you're excited about a new business idea, your RAS will highlight articles, conversations, and people that support your vision.

In other words, **your brain is constantly editing reality before you even see it.**

This explains why two people can walk through the same crowded street and notice completely different things. One sees danger, traffic, and noise. The other notices friendly faces, open shops, and new opportunities. They're in the same environment but their filters are tuned differently. Your RAS makes sure that what you focus on matches what you believe, whether that's empowering or limiting.

Imagine your Reticular Activating System as the bouncer at an exclusive nightclub; but instead of deciding who's on the guest list, it's deciding which bits of information get past the velvet rope into your conscious mind. Every sound, every face, every email notification is trying to get in, but the RAS only lets through what it thinks is "VIP."

It doesn't decide what's VIP on its own. *You* train it, often without even realizing it. The RAS takes its cues from your focus, your emotional state, and most importantly your underlying beliefs. If you've convinced yourself that people are generally cold or unfriendly, your RAS will scan every room for proof. You'll pick up on every annoyed glance, every curt reply, every stranger who doesn't hold the door. Meanwhile, the dozens of smiles or kind gestures simply don't make it past the door. Your brain doesn't register them as important.

Whereas, if your mind is focused on opportunities, your RAS will act like a spotlight, pointing them out everywhere. Ever notice how when you're hunting for a job, you suddenly "happen to overhear" conversations about openings, stumble on job posts online, or meet people who offer to help? That's not just luck, it's your brain flagging things it would normally ignore.

In other words, your brain isn't showing you reality as it actually is, it's showing you the version of reality that matches what you expect to see. The RAS is constantly sorting through the noise and handing you evidence to back up whatever story you're already telling yourself. Change the story, and you change what gets through the door.

Your RAS isn't just some background process you have no control over. It takes its marching orders from what you feed it. Every worry, every daydream, every goal you set, they're like little notes handed to your brain saying, *"This is important. Pay attention to this."*

The problem is, most of us program our RAS without even realizing it. If you're constantly worried about failing, your brain starts scanning for proof that you're in danger of messing up. A raised eyebrow from your boss feels like disapproval, one missed call feels like rejection, and every small setback looks like a disaster waiting to happen. It's not that the world suddenly got harsher; it's that your mental filter is tuned to threat.

You can train your RAS to work in your favor. By focusing deliberately on your goals, your strengths, and the outcomes you *want*, you teach your brain to filter for opportunities, ideas, and resources that help make those outcomes real.

Athletes have been using this trick for decades. Take a sprinter visualizing a perfect race or a golfer imagining the exact arc of a flawless swing. They're not just "thinking positive." They're literally conditioning their RAS to highlight anything that supports that vision - a training tip, a subtle movement, a chance to practice. It's like giving your brain a compass and saying, *"Point me towards this."*

The same applies outside of sports. Whether you're hunting for a new career, building a business, or simply wanting more joy in your day-to-day life, the signals you send your RAS determine what you notice and what you miss. If you don't set the program, your default worries and doubts will.

Now, here's where things get really interesting. Your RAS doesn't work in isolation. It's like the front desk to a much bigger operation: **your subconscious mind**. While your RAS decides what gets through to your conscious attention, your subconscious is the one supplying the guest list. It's holding on to your deepest beliefs, memories, and emotional patterns and those are what tell the RAS, *"Let this in. Ignore that."*

Say, for example, you carry an old belief that people don't really value you. Maybe it came from childhood experiences, maybe from a bad boss years ago. It doesn't matter where it started, your subconscious holds onto it. When you walk into a room, your RAS starts scanning faces for any hint of disapproval (a distracted glance, someone checking their phone) and feeds that to your conscious mind as *proof* you're not welcome.

Change this, and the opposite happens. If deep down you expect good things - that people like you, that opportunities are everywhere, your RAS highlights friendly smiles, helpful comments, and chance conversations. What you notice feels like "reality," but really it's your inner programming choosing what to spotlight.

This creates a powerful feedback loop. Your beliefs shape what you notice, what you notice reinforces those beliefs, and over time it becomes the lens through which you see the world. The good thing is that you can interrupt this cycle. Change the program your subconscious is running, and your RAS starts showing you a very different version of reality; one that supports where you want to go, not where you've been.

Neuroscientists studying attention have confirmed that the RAS is central to selective focus. In experiments, when participants were primed to look for certain patterns - whether images, words, or sounds, their RAS "lit up" and filtered everything else out. Similarly, research on goal-setting shows that clearly defined goals activate the RAS, essentially putting your brain on high alert for anything that relates to achieving them.

Modern neuroscience gives hard evidence for something people have intuitively known for centuries: *you notice what you're looking for.* Brain-imaging studies show that when people are told to watch for a specific image, word, or sound, the Reticular Activating System - that little bundle of neurons in your brainstem lights up like a switchboard. It automatically starts sifting through sensory overload, plucking out only what matches the brain's current priorities.

Goal-setting research echoes this. When you set a clear, specific goal your brain literally begins scanning your surroundings for anything that might help. It's why, once you decide to buy a certain type of car, you suddenly see it everywhere. That model was on the road all along, you just weren't tuned in.

This is more than coincidence or "positive thinking." It's your brain doing its job. Give it direction, and it will quietly rearrange your perception to match. Don't give it direction, and it defaults to whatever beliefs and fears you've been feeding it, even if those beliefs are outdated or self-sabotaging.

How to Train Your RAS in Daily Life

- **Set clear intentions.** Your brain needs specific instructions. "I want to feel healthier" is vague. "I'm looking for ways to improve my energy every day" gives your RAS something to track.
- **Use visualization.** Spending a few minutes each day imagining your ideal outcome programs your brain to notice opportunities that align with it.
- **Watch your inner dialogue.** If your self-talk is full of doubt, your RAS will serve you more of the same. Shift it towards curiosity, hope, and possibility.
- **Celebrate small wins.** Recognizing progress teaches your brain what's important, so it continues filtering for similar successes.

Chapter 8

Neuroplasticity - Rewiring the Brain for Change

For most of human history, scientists believed your brain was like hardened clay - once it set in early adulthood, that was it. Your personality, habits, and abilities were considered more or less permanent. If you weren't "naturally" good at math, if you struggled with confidence, or if you had a bad temper, that was simply your lot in life.

But over the past few decades, research has completely changed that idea. It turns out your brain isn't fixed at all. It's more like a bustling network of highways, always under construction. New routes are built. Old ones are widened when they're used often. And roads that are ignored eventually crumble and disappear.

This ability to change and adapt is called **neuroplasticity.**

In everyday terms, neuroplasticity means your brain can rewire itself not just when you're a child, but every single day of your life. Every thought you repeat, every skill you practice, every emotion you dwell on leaves a physical imprint. Neurons that "fire together" eventually wire together, forming stronger connections. The more often you travel the same mental path, the faster and smoother it becomes.

It's like walking through a field of tall grass. The first time it's tough - you're pushing stalks aside, unsure where to step. But walk that same path again and again, and soon a clear trail appears. Your brain works the same way. If you constantly think "I'm bad at public speaking," that becomes a well-worn mental path; so automatic that you barely notice it forming. But if you start practicing new thoughts, like "I'm learning to speak with confidence," you're carving a brand-new trail through the grass.

What's even more powerful is that neglected trails grow over. When you stop reinforcing old habits whether it's procrastination, self-doubt, or anger, those neural pathways gradually weaken. In other words, your brain is always in motion, either strengthening old patterns or building new ones.

This isn't just theory. MRI scans show real, physical changes in people who learn new skills, recover from injuries, or even shift their emotional patterns. Stroke patients have retrained their brains to control paralyzed limbs. Taxi drivers in London have been shown to develop larger brain areas for spatial navigation after years of memorizing the city's maze-like streets. And people who deliberately practice gratitude see measurable changes in brain regions linked to happiness and resilience.

Well, the bottom line is that you are not stuck being who you've always been. Your brain is under construction every day and you're holding the blueprints.

You know how some habits just feel automatic, almost like you're running on autopilot? That's because your brain is wired to take the easiest route. If you've been telling yourself "I'm not good enough" for years or reacting to stress by snapping at people, your brain has built a well-traveled path for that response. It's familiar, it's fast, and it doesn't even ask for your permission.

That wiring isn't permanent. You can build new paths. When you start doing things differently like taking a deep breath before losing your temper, or reminding yourself "I can figure this out" instead of "I always fail", you're slowly training your brain to go a different way. At first, it feels awkward and clunky, kind of like cutting a trail through tall grass. But keep walking that new path and it gets clearer and easier every time.

What about those old, negative paths? Well, they fade when you stop using them. Just like a dirt road grows over with weeds if no one drives on it, self-defeating habits lose their power when you stop giving them attention.

Think about learning to ride a bike. At first, you wobble all over the place. But after enough practice, your brain figures it out and suddenly you're cruising without thinking about it. Changing thought patterns works the same way. It's not about forcing yourself to be different forever, it's about practicing until the new way becomes second nature.

Real-World Proof of Change

Neuroplasticity isn't just some scientific buzzword, it's been proven in extraordinary and very practical ways. Take stroke patients, for example. When part of the brain is damaged, people can lose control of an arm, a leg, or even the ability to speak. For decades, doctors assumed that was permanent. But through therapy that forces patients to practice using the affected side, many of them actually regain movement. The brain literally rewires itself, assigning new areas to take over the lost function.

You see it in musicians too. Brain scans show that people who've spent years practicing an instrument have physically larger and more connected brain regions controlling finger movements and sound processing. Their dedication doesn't just improve skill, it reshapes their brain structure.

And it's not limited to physical abilities. People who've lived with chronic anxiety (constantly stuck in "fight or flight" mode) have learned to train their brains to calm down. Through practices like mindfulness or cognitive therapy, they've strengthened pathways linked to focus, resilience, and emotional balance. Over time, the "alarm bell" circuits quiet down, and the brain becomes wired for a calmer way of living.

Dr. Michael Merzenich, often called the "father of neuroplasticity," spent decades proving that the adult brain can reorganize itself even into old age. His work shows that learning a new language, picking up an instrument, or even training your memory doesn't just feel rewarding; it's like taking your brain to the gym. Just as muscles grow when you exercise, your brain builds new connections every time you challenge it with something unfamiliar.

The big takeaway from this is that change isn't limited by age or circumstance. Whether you're healing from an injury, learning a new skill at 60, or simply trying to break an old habit, your brain is capable of far more flexibility than we believe.

Your Thoughts Are Building Something

Think of your brain like a construction site that never shuts down. Every thought you repeat, every emotion you linger on, every belief you reinforce is like sending builders to work on that site. Worry rehearses anxiety pathways. Gratitude strengthens optimism circuits. Even visualizing a future goal builds mental blueprints and your brain treats it as practice for real life.

This isn't just a metaphor, it's literally how your brain works. When you practice something mentally or emotionally, your brain treats it like real-life rehearsal. That's why elite athletes spend time picturing the perfect shot or flawless performance; they're not just daydreaming, they're carving neurological "shortcuts" that make success easier to access under pressure.

This means that you're never stuck being who you've always been. You're not doomed to live with the same old habits, fears, or patterns forever. Your brain is constantly laying down new wiring, even when you're unaware of it. You're holding the blueprints, whether you realize it or not and every thought you repeat is a construction order.

If you keep telling yourself, *"I'm terrible with money,"* your brain reinforces the wiring for avoidance or panic around finances. But if you start telling yourself, *"I can learn to handle money,"* and you back that up with small consistent action, your brain starts building a new route. One that makes it easier to feel confident and in control.

You're never a finished product. You're a work in progress, and it means you can decide what the next version of you looks like.

CHAPTER 9

Altered States of Consciousness - Unlocking Creative and Healing Powers

Most of us spend our day in what's known as a **beta brainwave state.** Think of it as "daily life mode" - alert, logical, and focused on solving problems. You're planning your schedule, replying to messages, making decisions at work, and maybe juggling dinner plans in your head at the same time. Beta is useful for getting things done, but it can also make your mind feel like it's running on high speed - sharp, but sometimes a little too sharp. That's why prolonged beta often feels like overthinking, stress, or mental noise.

But your brain isn't stuck in just one gear. It naturally cycles through other **states of consciousness** during the day and these states aren't just random blips, they're windows of opportunity. They hold tremendous potential for creativity, insight, and even healing.

An altered state of consciousness isn't necessarily mystical or drug-induced (though some people explore it that way). You actually pass through altered states every day when you're drifting off to sleep, daydreaming, meditating, or "zoning out" on a walk.

In these states, your mind becomes less rigid and more open to new ideas, which is why creative breakthroughs often happen in the shower or right before bed. You slip in and out of these states every single day without even realizing it. Think about that drowsy feeling when you're just about to fall asleep, or the way you drift into a dream while staring out the bus window. Even those "aha!" moments in the shower happen because your mind has eased out of overdrive and into a softer, more open state.

These shifts can be measured by changes in your brain's electrical activity - what scientists call brainwave patterns. They're not abstract concepts; they're simply different speeds at which your brain processes information:

- **Beta (everyday alertness):** This is your "get stuff done" mode: focused, logical, and ready to solve problems. But living in beta all day long is like running your car at full speed. It burns fuel fast and often comes with stress, anxiety, and nonstop mental chatter.
- **Alpha (relaxed awareness):** You'll recognize alpha brainwaves if you've ever taken a slow walk in nature, listened to music that puts you in a good mood, or simply sat back and let your thoughts flow without pressure. Alpha feels calm but awake - like your brain is still sharp, just less tense.
- **Theta (deep relaxation and creativity):** Theta is where your mind starts to wander into the subconscious. It's the twilight zone between wakefulness and sleep, where daydreams, vivid imagery, and creative ideas surface with little effort. Hypnosis, guided meditation, and those moments when you're "in the zone" all tap into theta waves. In this state, your subconscious is wide open to suggestion, making it powerful for reprogramming old patterns or sparking fresh ideas.
- **Delta (deep sleep and healing):** Delta waves are the slowest, and they dominate when you're in deep, dreamless sleep. This is when your body repairs itself, your immune system strengthens,

and your brain clears out waste. It's like a nightly maintenance cycle. Without enough delta, both your mind and body feel drained.

What's fascinating is that these aren't separate worlds, they're gears your brain naturally shifts through. But most of us get stuck in beta for far too long, running from one task to the next, rarely dipping into the richer, slower rhythms where insight, creativity, and healing thrive.

Why These States Matter

When you're locked in beta mode all day, your conscious, analytical mind dominates. But in alpha and theta states, the subconscious becomes more accessible; meaning you can plant new ideas, release old patterns, and access intuitive insights.

Most of us spend our days revving the mental engine in beta mode - solving problems, meeting deadlines, responding to notifications. It's useful for getting things done, but it keeps us operating from the conscious, analytical part of the brain. That's great for balancing your checkbook or writing an email, but not so great for deep insight, creativity, or changing subconscious patterns.

When you shift into **alpha** or **theta**, something remarkable happens: your brainwaves slow down, your inner critic relaxes, and your subconscious becomes far more open to suggestion and change. These states are like opening a door to the "control room" of your mind, where the real programming happens.

This is why meditation, hypnosis, or even just daydreaming can feel so powerful. You're no longer fighting uphill against your own mental resistance. Instead, you're planting seeds directly into fertile soil.

History is full of people who've used this to their advantage. **Thomas Edison** famously used his light-drowsy state as a creative tool. He'd sit holding steel balls in his hands while dozing in a chair.

As soon as he slipped into that half-asleep theta state, his muscles would relax, the balls would drop, and the noise would wake him. He'd quickly jot down the flashes of insight that surfaced before his analytical mind fully took over. **Salvador Dalí**, the surrealist painter, used the exact same trick for dreamlike inspiration.

You've probably experienced this yourself: a solution to a stubborn problem pops up in the shower, on a long walk, or just as you're nodding off to sleep. That's not coincidence, it's your brain shifting gears into a state where it can connect dots in ways your conscious mind can't.

Alpha and theta aren't just "relaxing", they're practical tools. They allow you to rewire old thought patterns, boost creativity, and access insights that feel almost magical because they bypass your usual mental filters.

It's not just about creativity. Studies show meditation, hypnosis, and deep relaxation can lower blood pressure, reduce chronic pain, and speed up recovery from illness. When the mind shifts into slower brainwave states, stress hormones decrease and the body's natural repair mechanisms kick in.

Altered states of consciousness aren't just tools for creative breakthroughs, they have a measurable impact on physical health and healing. When your brain shifts from the fast, stressed beta waves of everyday life into slower alpha, theta, or even delta rhythms, your entire physiology changes. Stress hormones like cortisol drop, heart rate and blood pressure stabilize, and the body's built-in repair systems switch on.

This isn't just theory. **Dozens of studies show that practices like meditation, guided imagery, deep breathing, and hypnosis can accelerate recovery, relieve chronic pain, and even improve immune function.** Hospitals today use these methods alongside conventional medicine, not as "alternative" treatments, but because they work.

Consider how **hypnosis is used in medicine**. In some documented cases, patients have had dental surgery, wound care, and even childbirth with little or no chemical anesthesia. By entering a deeply focused, altered state, their perception of pain changed so dramatically that what should have been unbearable became manageable. This isn't magic or mind-over-matter in the mystical sense, it's the brain literally changing how it interprets and processes signals from the body.

You've probably felt a hint of this before. Think about a time you were completely absorbed in a good book or movie and didn't notice a headache until the credits rolled. Or when you were so nervous before speaking in public that your stomach hurt and then felt fine as soon as it was over. These are everyday examples of how brain states influence what the body feels.

When we intentionally enter relaxed, receptive states, we give the body permission to heal. Whether through meditation, breathing exercises, yoga, or guided hypnosis, you're quieting the mental noise that keeps your nervous system on high alert and allowing balance to return.

Tapping Into These States Intentionally

You don't need to be a monk or mystic to use these states.

- **Meditation and breathing exercises** can guide you into alpha and theta, where you can reprogram old beliefs.
- **Guided imagery or visualization** can help you rehearse success, strengthen motivation, or support healing.
- **Mindful hobbies** like painting, music, or walking in nature naturally quiet the analytical mind and open creative channels.

The key is learning how to shift gears on purpose instead of waiting for inspiration to "strike."

Chapter 10

Autosuggestion and Affirmations - Rewriting Your Inner Script

We all live with a constant voice in our heads. A running commentary that judges, predicts, and labels everything we do. Sometimes it cheers us on. More often, it doubts us, nitpicks our flaws, or replays old criticisms from parents, teachers, or past failures.

The problem is that your subconscious mind doesn't argue with that voice. It simply absorbs whatever it hears most often and treats it as fact. Like a personal assistant that never questions your orders, it keeps arranging your thoughts, emotions, and behaviors to match the story you've been telling yourself.

Autosuggestion and affirmations are tools to change that story on purpose. Instead of letting outdated beliefs run on autopilot, you install new, empowering instructions - ones that shape your decisions, energy, and focus in ways that actually serve you.

What Exactly Is Autosuggestion?

Autosuggestion is the practice of deliberately feeding your mind specific, repeated messages until they sink into your subconscious and begin shaping your reality. It's not wishful thinking, it's more like training your brain to expect and create better outcomes.

The concept was first brought into the spotlight by French psychologist and pharmacist Émile Coué in the early 1900s. Coué noticed something remarkable: when patients believed they would recover, they often healed faster and responded better to treatment even when the medicine itself was nothing special. To help his patients cultivate that sense of expectation, he taught them to repeat a simple line, several times a day and with real feeling:

"Every day, in every way, I'm getting better and better."

It may sound almost too simple, but Coué wasn't claiming it was magic. What he found was that when people consistently tell themselves something with conviction, their subconscious begins to accept it as fact. And when your subconscious accepts an idea, your choices, behavior, and even your body begin to follow that script automatically.

Try and think about it. If you spend your day telling yourself, "I'm terrible at this, nothing ever works out for me," your brain will happily go to work proving you right. You'll notice every mistake, overlook your progress, and shy away from opportunities because you're sure you'll fail anyway. But when you change this to something like "I'm improving every day; I'm capable of figuring this out" your brain starts scanning for evidence to support that belief instead. You become more relaxed, more willing to try again, and more likely to notice solutions you'd otherwise miss.

Even modern research echoes what Coué discovered over a century ago. People who use positive self-talk under pressure - whether athletes before a competition or patients recovering from injuries tend to perform better, recover faster, and stay calmer. It's not that a few words magically change reality; it's that they gradually train your mind to see and respond to reality in a different way.

Imagine two people learning to play guitar. One mutters, "I'm so clumsy; I'll never get this right." The other says, "I'm getting better every time I pick this up." Both may be starting at the same skill level, but the second person stays patient, keeps practicing, and actually improves faster. Why? Because his subconscious is being programmed to expect progress rather than failure and that expectation subtly guides how his brain and body approach the task.

Why Affirmations Work. And Why They Sometimes Don't

Affirmations are simply intentional statements you feed to your mind to shift your beliefs and guide your behavior. They're like verbal seeds. The more often you plant and water them, the more they take root in your subconscious. Examples might sound like:

"I handle challenges calmly and clearly."
"I deserve to be paid well for my skills."
"I attract supportive people into my life."

Over time, repeating these messages reshapes the way you see yourself and the world. But, your brain can't be bullied into believing something totally unrealistic.

If you're flat-out broke and you look in the mirror saying, *"I'm a millionaire right now!"* your inner voice might laugh, roll its eyes, and mutter, *"Yeah, sure you are."* When there's a too-big gap between what you're saying and what you actually believe, your subconscious rejects the message.

A better way is to start where you are, with affirmations you can actually get behind. Instead of jumping straight to *"I'm rich,"* you might affirm:

"I'm learning how to manage my money and open new opportunities."
or
"Each day, I'm getting better at creating financial stability."

These kinds of statements feel real enough that your subconscious won't fight them. They represent progress instead of pretending you're already at the finish line. And once your subconscious buys into these smaller, believable steps, it begins scanning your environment for proof: spotting opportunities, resources, and ideas you might have ignored before.

Think of it like building a staircase rather than trying to pole-vault to the top. Start with a step you can stand on, and your brain will help you climb higher. Small shifts in belief create momentum, and momentum changes everything.

You've probably experienced this without even realizing it. Have you ever decided, *"I need to start eating healthier,"* and suddenly you notice healthy recipes, grocery sales, or fitness advice everywhere? That's your mind aligning with your intention and affirmations work in a similar way.

Boxing legend **Muhammad Ali** mastered the art of autosuggestion. Long before he became world champion, he repeated to himself and to anyone who would listen:

"I am the greatest!"

These weren't empty words. Ali was training his subconscious as much as his body. By affirming his greatness, he created an unshakable belief system; one that guided his training, his attitude in the ring, and his refusal to give up when things got tough. His words became reality because they shaped the way he acted long before the world agreed with him.

Your subconscious doesn't care whether a message comes from you or from someone else. It doesn't stop to ask whether something is true. I=t just soaks up whatever it hears often, especially if it's said with feeling. It doesn't matter if the words come from you, someone else, or even a TV ad. If it's repeated enough, it sticks.

That's why offhand comments from childhood can echo for years. And that is why catchy jingles get stuck in your head, and harsh self-talk starts to feel real; not because it *is* real, but because your mind has practiced it so many times.

Since your subconscious learns through repetition, you can decide what to feed it. Keep repeating something supportive, and over time the old noise gets quieter. "I can't do this" gradually turns into "I'm learning how to do this."

Small, steady turns change the whole course. The more you guide your thoughts in the direction you want, the more your subconscious follows along.

But this also means **you can take control of what gets programmed.** By deliberately repeating empowering thoughts, you drown out the old noise and give your subconscious new instructions to follow.

For affirmations and autosuggestions to work, they need:

1. **Consistency** - You can't tell your brain something once and expect it to rewire. Daily repetition matters.
2. **Emotion** - The subconscious pays attention to feelings more than dry words. Saying it with conviction; even imagining the relief or excitement of it being true makes it stick.
3. **Visualization** - Pairing affirmations with mental images super-charges the effect. When you *see* yourself acting confident or achieving a goal, your brain treats it like practice.
4. **Present Tense** - Speak as though it's already happening. "I am learning…" or "I am becoming…" signals your brain to start aligning now, not someday.

Using autosuggestion isn't about lying to yourself or pretending everything's perfect. It's more like giving your brain better instructions. If you've been telling yourself, "I'm unlucky," or "I can't do anything right," that's just old programming running on repeat; and like any software, you can update it.

When you start feeding yourself better messages, like "I'm figuring things out," or "I'm getting better at this every day," you gradually shift how you see yourself. You walk into situations with more confidence, you make different choices, and people start picking up on that change too.

It doesn't happen overnight. But after a few weeks or months, you'll notice something interesting, subtle and powerful. Your reality begins to match your words.

PART 2

The Nature of Reality

Chapter 11

Time Beyond the Clock: Altered Timelines and Déjà Vu

Time is supposed to be simple; or at least that's what the clock on your phone would have you believe. One second ticks after another, hours roll into days, and days turn into years. We're told the past is behind us, the present is all we have, and the future hasn't happened yet. It sounds neat and orderly… but life keeps dropping clues that it's not so straightforward.

Have you ever met someone for the very first time, yet felt an instant familiarity, as if you'd known them for years? Or walked into a building you've never visited and had the unsettling feeling that you've been there before? Maybe you've had those strange gaps while driving, when you suddenly "snap back" and realize you can't remember the last ten minutes of the road.

These moments feel random, but they hint at something bigger: time doesn't always behave like the rigid, linear ruler we think it is. Our minds seem to slip in and out of ordinary awareness, catching glimpses of something beyond the tick-tock of the clock.

What's fascinating is that science, spirituality, and everyday human experience are all starting to align on this point.

Neuroscientists studying how we perceive time, philosophers questioning its nature, and spiritual teachers talking about timeless awareness are all circling the same idea: our sense of time is flexible. And it may be more connected to consciousness than we ever imagined.

The first crack in the idea of fixed, mechanical time is right in front of us. We simply don't experience it evenly. Ten minutes waiting for a dentist appointment can feel like torture, stretching out forever. Yet ten minutes spent laughing with friends at dinner can vanish in what feels like a blink. Athletes describe moments of being "in the zone," where the game seems to slow to half-speed, allowing them to make decisions with impossible precision. People who've had near misses - a car accident narrowly avoided, a sudden fall often report the same thing: *time itself seemed to freeze.*

Neuroscientists have found there's no single "clock" in the brain keeping precise time. Instead, your sense of time is constructed on the fly, using attention, memory, and emotion as raw material. When you're bored or anxious, your mind keeps checking in, slicing time into tiny pieces and making each second feel longer. When you're fully immersed, your brain stops measuring time altogether, so the hours disappear unnoticed.

But here's where things get interesting. What if these distortions aren't *just* tricks of perception? What if they're small clues that time itself is more flexible than we've been taught? Modern physics already tells us that time isn't absolute, it bends and stretches with speed and gravity. And on a human scale, consciousness seems to interact with time in strange ways. The moments when time feels slower or faster might not just be glitches in your brain's stopwatch, they could be windows into how fluid time really is.

Déjà Vu: A Glitch, a Glimpse, or Something Deeper?

Déjà vu - that uncanny sense that you've already experienced a moment is one of those universal mysteries. Almost everyone has felt it. You're in mid-conversation, and suddenly every gesture, every word feels eerily familiar. You step into a café you've never been to, but something inside whispers, *I know this place.* The moment passes in seconds, leaving you both unsettled and oddly curious.

Mainstream neuroscience explains déjà vu as a hiccup in memory processing. Your brain takes in information through different channels - sight, sound, emotion and normally syncs it up in real time. But sometimes these signals arrive slightly out of order. One part of your brain processes the scene a fraction of a second before another, creating a false sense of recognition. Brain scans show that during déjà vu, the **temporal lobe**, the same region that handles memory, suddenly lights up as if you're recalling something, even though there's nothing to recall.

It's a neat explanation, but it feels incomplete. If déjà vu is just a wiring glitch, why do so many people describe it as meaningful? Why do some moments of déjà vu carry a deep emotional charge, as if the universe itself is nudging you?

Some researchers believe déjà vu might be less of an "error" and more of a pattern match. Your subconscious mind stores immense amounts of information - fragments of dreams, intuitions, fleeting impressions and far more than you can consciously track. When something in the present lines up with one of these buried patterns, you feel an uncanny familiarity. In other words, your brain may be whispering, *We've run this scenario before.*

This could explain why déjà vu often occurs during transitional moments - meeting someone new, visiting unfamiliar places, or making a big decision. Your subconscious may be flagging these moments as significant, pushing them into sharper focus.

But there's an even more intriguing possibility. What if déjà vu isn't *just* a quirk of memory, but a hint that time itself isn't as rigid as we think? Some physicists describe time not as a flowing river, but as a landscape where past, present, and future all exist at once, and our consciousness simply moves through it like a traveler walking a path. In that view, déjà vu might be a moment when you "jump ahead on the trail" for just an instant or briefly remember where you've already been.

Spiritual traditions have echoed this for centuries. In Hindu and Buddhist teachings, déjà vu is sometimes interpreted as evidence of reincarnation or karmic patterns repeating across lifetimes. In Western mysticism, it's seen as a sign you're aligned with your "soul path" crossing milestones you were always meant to encounter.

Even modern psychology can't dismiss how powerfully déjà vu feels. People often report a strange *rightness* about it, as if the moment is exactly where they're supposed to be. Could it be your inner compass recognizing something your conscious mind can't yet explain?

Altered Timelines and "Time Slips"

Déjà vu might be one piece of a bigger puzzle: moments when our usual sense of time bends, loops, or even rewrites itself. Around the world, there are countless stories of "time slips"; episodes where people feel they've briefly stepped into another era or timeline.

- **In 1979**, two English couples driving through rural France reported spending the night at an old-fashioned inn with oil lamps, horse-drawn carts outside, and staff in period clothing. When they tried to return a few days later, the inn was gone and no records of it ever existed.
- **During World War I**, soldiers in Flanders reported watching an entire medieval battle unfold on the same ground where they were fighting, then vanish as suddenly as it appeared.
- **Even in everyday life**, people describe "missing time" like driving a familiar route and suddenly realizing they've covered miles with no memory of it.

Skeptics chalk these events up to misremembered details, stress, or tricks of perception. But what if they're hints that time is not a single, unbending line, but something more like a fabric, with folds, overlaps, and alternate threads?

Physicists exploring **quantum mechanics** and **multiverse theories** are starting to take such ideas more seriously. If reality is layered, if countless possible timelines exist, then déjà vu and time slips might be moments where those layers brush against each other.

What if déjà vu isn't just your brain misfiring, but a signal that your life doesn't always unfold in a straight line? Imagine time not as a single track, but as a web of winding paths, splitting and reconnecting in ways too complex to see from ground level.

In this view, déjà vu might be your consciousness brushing up against another path - one where you've already been here, already made this choice, already seen this moment play out. That's why it doesn't just feel familiar. It feels significant, like a subtle tap saying: *Pay attention. This matters.*

Reports of these strange overlaps are everywhere. A man traveling through Spain took a wrong turn into a narrow alley and suddenly found himself walking among people dressed in fashions from the 1940s. The cars, the storefronts, even the music playing on a crackling radio were all from a different era. When he returned minutes later with a friend, the alley was modern again. No trace of the past.

A woman in New York stepped into an old bookstore and spoke with a kindly gray-haired shopkeeper who recommended a rare novel. When she went back the next day to buy it, the building was boarded up. Locals told her the shop had closed years ago and the man she described had passed away.

These experiences are often dismissed as tricks of memory or imagination. Yet their consistency is striking. People in different cultures, different times, tell remarkably similar stories: walking into a place that shouldn't exist anymore, meeting people who seem to have stepped out of another century, or sensing information about someone they logically couldn't know.

What if these aren't coincidences, but glimpses of alternate threads of reality? Physics already tells us that time and space are not rigid, they're part of a flexible fabric that can bend, stretch, and even overlap. If space can curve, why not time? And if time has layers, maybe our awareness can sometimes slip between them.

Déjà vu could be a small taste of this. Perhaps it's not "remembering the past," but momentarily syncing up with another version of yourself who has already **lived this event**.

Why This Changes Everything

If these experiences hint at altered timelines, they carry a powerful message: **the future isn't fixed.** You are not walking down a single predestined road. Instead, you're moving through a landscape of possibilities and your subconscious mind might be catching glimpses of routes your conscious mind hasn't reached yet.

That instant familiarity when meeting someone new? Maybe, in another branch of time, you've shared years of history.

That powerful nudge to make a certain decision? Maybe it's your inner compass sensing the path where you thrive.

That feeling you've "seen this before"? Maybe you have. Just not in *this* exact version of reality.

These aren't just curious moments to laugh off. They may be signs that you're far more connected to the deeper structure of existence than you realize.

If time isn't rigid, déjà vu and "time slips" aren't random glitches. They're tiny markers that you're brushing against the edges of something bigger, something layered and alive.

Some physicists describe time as a landscape where past, present, and future all coexist, while consciousness moves through it like a traveler on a winding trail. In this model, déjà vu may be a moment when you step slightly off the main path and catch sight of where other trails run parallel.

The real question isn't *"Is this real?"* but *"What is it showing me?"* If you can sense these overlaps even for a second, it suggests that your awareness isn't bound to the ticking hands of a clock. Reality itself may be far more flexible, and far more responsive to you, than you've been led to believe.

What if déjà vu isn't just your brain messing up? What if it's your mind remembering the way things were *before something changed*?

Picture your life as a road. You think it goes straight, but sometimes, without realizing it, the road quietly forks and you take a different turn. Maybe it's because of a choice you made, someone else's decision, or even events far outside your control. Most of the time, the shift is smooth; you don't notice anything. But sometimes a tiny part of you remembers the "old route." When you reach the same moment again on this new path, you get that sudden jolt of familiarity: **déjà vu.**

How does that happen?

Think of reality as a giant web made of many threads. If one thread gets pulled, the whole pattern changes slightly. Usually, you only see the final version, like a story that's been edited before you read it. But now and then, your mind catches a faint memory of the earlier draft; the way things were just a moment ago; and it feels like you've already lived this.

It's like when you rewrite a document on your computer. You fix one sentence, and suddenly the whole page shifts. You don't see the old version anymore, but you *remember* it being different. Déjà vu is that tiny memory surfacing - your brain whispering: *"Hey, something just changed."*

Why does it feel so strong?

This is why déjà vu often comes with a strange weight, as if the moment really matters.

- Meet someone new and feel like you've known them for years? Maybe in another version of events, you did.
- Walk into a place you've never been, but it feels familiar? Maybe you were there, just not in this exact timeline.
- Make a choice that feels "already decided"? Maybe part of you remembers choosing it once already.

If time can bend and rewrite itself, déjà vu isn't a glitch, it's a signal. It's your deeper awareness poking through, reminding you that life isn't locked in a straight line. You're not stuck watching events roll by, you're inside a story that can still change.

That two-second shiver of recognition may be your mind brushing against the edges of reality, catching an echo of what came before.

Imagine life like a movie that's constantly being edited while you're watching it. Most of the time, the edits are seamless; you never notice the cuts. But sometimes, when something major changes - a choice you make, a decision someone else makes, or even something you can't see, it's as if the scene has been rewritten.

You keep watching the "new version," but somewhere deep in your mind, a trace of the old scene remains. That faint memory of what "used to be" can pop up as déjà vu.

Why You Get Glimpses

Your subconscious mind holds far more information than your conscious mind. If reality really can shift even slightly, your subconscious may feel the change first. That's why déjà vu feels like *knowing* instead of just remembering. It's not that you read about this moment in a book; it's that you somehow *lived it already*, in a version of events that just got edited out.

So What Does This Mean?

If déjà vu happens when timelines shift, it suggests your life isn't set in stone.

- The future is flexible.
- The past may be more fluid than we think.
- And every choice you make could quietly bend reality in a new direction.

Rather than being something to ignore, déjà vu could be a gentle signal from your deeper self: *Pay attention. You're standing at a crossroads and this moment matters.*

Think of it like when you edit a photo on your phone. You crop it, adjust the colors, maybe erase a blemish. The new picture looks perfect, but if you've ever seen the original, you can't quite forget what it looked like before the edit.

Life might work the same way. Imagine reality making a tiny "edit" maybe because of a choice you made, or even one you haven't noticed yet. You keep living inside the updated version, but a part of your mind remembers the original for just a split second. That's when déjà vu hits. Like your brain whispering, *"I've seen this scene before… but it wasn't quite like this."*

If time isn't strictly linear, then the future may not be fixed and the past may not be entirely gone. Déjà vu could be a subtle reminder that your consciousness is capable of more than simply marking seconds on a clock. It might be glimpsing a roadmap, or tuning into parallel versions of reality.

This chapter lays the foundation for what comes next.

Modern physics has already shaken up our simple view of time. Einstein's theory of relativity showed that time isn't constant, it bends with speed and gravity. Astronauts on the International Space Station age ever so slightly slower than people on Earth because of these effects. In quantum mechanics, particles sometimes behave as though future events can influence their present behavior - a phenomenon called "retrocausality."

Now, this doesn't mean you'll suddenly remember next week's winning lottery numbers. But it does mean the idea of time as a strict past→present→future conveyor belt isn't accurate. Time is more like a landscape and consciousness might not be limited to walking through it step by step.

This opens the door to strange but intriguing possibilities. If time is a field rather than a straight line, maybe déjà vu isn't a mistake. Maybe it's a momentary peek at how your consciousness can move through that field in ways you're not fully aware of.

Long before modern science caught on, humans sensed that the mind can step outside ordinary time. Ancient shamans, mystics, and philosophers described visions of the future or glimpses of past lives. Today, we talk about it more cautiously - as intuition, gut feelings, or dreams that come true. But the mechanism might be similar: when your conscious mind quiets down, your subconscious can access information outside your usual "now."

Think of how vividly imagining a future goal can change you. When you picture it over and over, not just as a wish, but as something real and detailed, your brain responds as though it's already happening. Neural pathways fire. Your emotions shift. You notice opportunities that match your vision, because your attention is primed. In a sense, you're borrowing feelings and behaviors from your future self.

On the other hand, when you obsess over fears or regrets, you're mentally living in the past or future in a way that shapes your present. Your subconscious doesn't know the difference, it reacts as though the danger or disappointment is happening now.

This ability to "time travel" internally is built into you. And it hints at something profound: the boundary between past, present, and future may be more porous than we realize.

Why does this matter? Because understanding how flexible time can be helps explain some of life's strangest experiences and sets the stage for what comes next. Déjà vu might be more than a curiosity. Those moments when you "just know" something is going to happen, or when your dreams play out in waking life, might not be accidents at all.

If your consciousness can interact with time in non-linear ways, even briefly, it could also explain phenomena like intuition, premonitions, and what some call "parallel timelines." In the next chapters, we'll explore these possibilities not as science fiction, but as clues to how reality itself might work.

Chapter 12

Parallel Universes

What if the world you see isn't the only one? What if right now, as you read these words, another version of you is making different choices - living a life that feels both distant and strangely familiar?

This isn't just the stuff of science fiction movies. Increasingly, scientists, philosophers, and mystics are starting to talk about reality in surprisingly similar ways. The idea is bold. We may live in a universe that's not singular, but layered. Countless realities stacked side by side, each branching off when decisions are made, events shift, or possibilities unfold.

In quantum physics, reality at its smallest scale doesn't behave the way we expect. The tiniest building blocks of the universe (particles like electrons and photons) don't act like little billiard balls rolling neatly along a table. Instead, they behave like clouds of possibilities. A particle can be here and there at the same time, spinning both clockwise and anti-clockwise, existing in multiple states at once. This strange condition is called *superposition.*

But the moment we measure or observe a particle, it "collapses" into one definite state - one position, one direction, one outcome. For decades, scientists wondered: *why does nature seem to make a single choice only when we look?*

In 1957, a young physicist named Hugh Everett offered a bold answer: "*maybe nature never makes just one choice at all.*" What if every possible outcome actually happens, just not in the same universe? According to his "Many Worlds Interpretation," when a particle is in superposition, reality itself splits. One universe shows one result. Another universe shows the other. Both continue to exist, side by side, like parallel pages in an infinite book.

At first, this idea sounded outrageous. But over time, it began to solve problems other theories couldn't. Quantum experiments kept showing that particles behaved as if they really *did* live in multiple realities until observed. Everett's view simply takes this at face value: every possible event plays out somewhere.

Imagine life like an endlessly branching tree. Every decision - big or small is a fork in the road. Take one job here, and in another branch you take a different job. Say yes to a date tonight, and in another version of reality you stayed home instead. Nothing gets erased. The other branches don't vanish, you just continue along one path while countless others grow alongside it.

To you, it feels like there's only one "you," moving forward in one straight line. But what if your mind occasionally senses these other paths? Could déjà vu, gut feelings, or uncanny coincidences be tiny leaks between worlds - moments when the branches brush close together?

Some scientists and philosophers even wonder if consciousness itself isn't locked to a single timeline. If reality is constantly branching, maybe part of you deep down is aware of other outcomes. That nagging feeling of "I've been here before" might not be an illusion at all. It might be the echo of another you who's already lived that moment.

Long before quantum physics gave us words like "superposition" or "many worlds," spiritual traditions were already pointing to something similar. In Hindu philosophy, the universe is described as *maya* - not "fake," but a shifting dream where reality is layered, flexible, and far deeper than it appears. In Buddhist thought, countless realms of existence are said to overlap with ours, visible only when consciousness is quiet and clear. Many Native American traditions speak of "dream worlds" running beside the waking one, places you can visit in visions, where life unfolds differently yet feels strangely connected to this one.

Mystics and shamans from every culture have told stories of moments when the curtain of ordinary life thins. In deep meditation, intense prayer, or even in dreams, they report glimpses of other landscapes, other versions of events as though they've briefly stepped sideways into another thread of reality. Sufi poets wrote of the world as a woven fabric, with countless hidden strands intersecting at mysterious points. Indigenous elders described life as a circle, not a straight line, where different paths can touch, separate, and touch again.

What's remarkable is how closely these descriptions echo what modern science now suggests in a completely different language. Quantum physics describes reality not as one solid block, but as a spectrum of probabilities. **A living web of possibilities that only looks fixed because we're usually seeing just one strand at a time.** What ancient wisdom called divine mystery, science now calls probability, superposition, and parallel outcomes.

Both are saying the same thing in different ways: **what we take as "the world" is just one version among many.**

So what does all this talk of parallel worlds have to do with you? More than you might think. If parallel realities exist, your life isn't a single straight road with no exits. It's more like using GPS with multiple suggested routes; all starting at the same point but ending up in slightly (or wildly) different places. You're currently driving on one route, but that doesn't mean the others don't exist. They're running alongside, just on different streets.

Most of the time, you're focused on the road you're on. But sometimes, you catch a glimpse of another route; maybe a street sign, maybe a shortcut you recognize even though you've never taken it. Déjà vu might be your mind catching one of those glimpses: a sense that you've already been here, not on *this* path, but on another one running close by.

Dreams that later come true, sudden flashes of recognition with strangers, or the feeling that a moment is strangely familiar. These could all be tiny overlaps where different "routes" of your life briefly line up, and you sense more than one version of yourself moving through time.

An unshakable sense that you "almost remember" a moment as it's happening; these might be brief leaks between realities.

Picture this: you're standing at a career crossroads. In one timeline, you take a leap of faith and start your own business. In another, you stay at your steady job. You can't live both at once. At least not consciously. But somewhere deep inside, you might *feel* the presence of both paths. It might show up as a powerful intuition, an idea that feels "too real" to ignore, or a strange sense of familiarity when you imagine your future.

Some people describe these moments like quiet nudges from another version of themselves. A reminder that there's more than one way your story can unfold. And while you normally only see one outcome, these glimpses hint that your life is part of something far richer and more interconnected than you realize.

If parallel universes are real, the next big question is: are they completely sealed off from each other, or can they occasionally interact?

Most of the time, each version of reality would run on its own track. But some physicists speculate that under certain conditions, moments we don't yet fully understand - those tracks might come close enough to touch.

Imagine reality as a vast, flexible fabric. If that fabric folds or ripples, two layers could briefly brush against each other. When that happens, the edges might blur and we might feel it. Maybe that's what's behind some of the strangest human experiences:

- **Meeting a stranger who seems to know you deeply** and can't explain why.
- **Objects appearing in odd places**, with no logical reason for how they got there.
- **Sudden, overwhelming intuition**, like knowing what someone will say before they speak or feeling you've already lived this moment before.

Are these coincidences? Or are they tiny leaks in the cosmic wall, where another version of reality drifts close enough for you to sense it?

Whether you interpret this as science, spirituality, or a blend of both, the message is profound:

> **You are not confined to one rigid story.** Life may not be a single straight track but a landscape of possibilities.
>
> **Reality is far more fluid than we've been taught.** If multiple outcomes exist, then the idea of "fate" becomes less like a locked door and more like a set of open hallways.
>
> **Your choices might ripple farther than you can imagine.** Even small decisions could echo through the web of possibilities in ways we don't yet understand.

If every path exists somewhere, then there's no ultimate failure; only different experiences. Your job isn't to pick the "perfect" path but to choose the one that feels most alive, most aligned, in *this* moment.

Chapter 13

Premonitions and Prophetic Insights

Have you ever just *known* something before it happened? Maybe you thought of an old friend out of nowhere, and they called you an hour later. Or you had a sudden, uneasy feeling about taking a certain road, only to hear later there was an accident there. Some people brush these moments off as coincidence. Others call them luck, intuition, or even divine guidance. But what if they're none of those; or perhaps all of them at once?

Throughout history, people have reported premonitions - flashes of insight about events that haven't yet occurred. Sometimes they come as subtle nudges: a quiet thought you can't shake, a vivid dream that lingers in your mind. Other times they arrive as powerful, crystal-clear visions of things to come. These experiences are so common that almost everyone has at least one story.

Modern science often explains them away as chance, memory errors, or selective attention. We remember the hits and forget the misses. Yet, there's growing evidence that something deeper might be happening. If time isn't a single straight line; if reality is layered with overlapping paths, as we saw with déjà vu and parallel universes, then maybe premonitions are brief glimpses of where those paths are leading.

The human brain is an incredible prediction machine. Even in ordinary life, your subconscious constantly scans for patterns. It notices tiny details you don't consciously register; like a flicker in someone's voice, a shift in the weather, an unfamiliar tension in your body and uses them to make lightning-fast guesses about what's coming next. Sometimes those guesses are so accurate, they feel supernatural.

Most of the time, we don't even realize this is happening. You just "get a feeling" about someone's mood before they say a word. You "sense" that it's going to rain before checking the forecast. And often, these little insights are so spot-on that they feel uncanny.

But then there are the other cases. The ones that don't fit neatly into psychology or common sense. The dream about a plane crash that matches the morning news. The sudden urge to call a loved one, only to find out they needed you at that exact moment. The creeping dread that pulls someone out of a building just before disaster strikes. These aren't just subtle guesses your brain stitched together from cues; they feel like something else entirely.

This is where science itself starts to stumble. For decades, researchers studying time perception have run experiments with surprising results. In some studies, participants were hooked up to machines measuring their physiological responses; things like heart rate, electrical skin activity, and nervous system reactions. The participants were shown a series of images on a screen: some neutral (a chair, a tree, a cup), and some highly emotional (a violent scene, a car accident, an affectionate embrace).

In several experiments, people's bodies reacted *before* the emotional image appeared, sometimes by a second or two. Their heart rates jumped, their skin conductance spiked, as though they were preparing for something their conscious minds could not see yet. Statistically, the results shouldn't have been possible if time was only a one-way street.

It's as if a part of the mind was already standing in tomorrow while the rest of it was still in today.

This doesn't mean we all have crystal-clear visions of the future. More likely, it means our awareness isn't as tightly locked into the present moment as we've been taught. Some part of us may reach a little further, brushing against events just ahead on the timeline. Think of it like catching an echo before the sound arrives, or seeing the faint glow of headlights before the car rounds the corner.

Could this explain why premonitions often come through dreams, gut feelings, or sudden flashes of knowing? These are the states where our conscious, logical mind quiets down, giving space for the subtler signals of the subconscious, or perhaps even the deeper fabric of time itself to slip through.

If the future isn't fixed, if there are different versions of how things could play out, then premonitions might just be those moments when you accidentally peek ahead. It's like catching a trailer for a movie before the full thing is released.

Well, life isn't one straight road. It's more like a whole network of roads twisting and crossing each other. Most of the time, you're just walking on your chosen road, focused on what's right in front of you. But every now and then, something strange happens. You catch a glimpse of another road running alongside yours. Maybe it comes as a dream, maybe as a gut feeling, or maybe just as a quick thought that feels "too real" to ignore.

This is where déjà vu and premonitions connect. Déjà vu might be you brushing against a moment you've already lived, but on a slightly different version of your road. Premonitions could be you leaning a little forward in time, seeing a step or two before you actually get there. Either way, it suggests your mind isn't as locked into the present moment as we usually assume.

And just because you saw or felt something doesn't mean it's set in stone. Maybe you dreamed of an accident, but when the day comes, something nudges you to turn left instead of right and suddenly you're on a different road. The "preview" you got was real, but it was only one of the many routes your life could've taken.

So instead of thinking of premonitions as scary predictions, maybe it's better to see them as reminders that you're connected to more possibilities than you realize.

History is full of strange premonitions that make us pause.

One of the most famous comes from **Abraham Lincoln**. Just days before his assassination, he told close friends about a vivid dream. He wandered through the White House, hearing muffled sobs. Entering a room, he saw a coffin surrounded by soldiers. When he asked who had died, a guard replied, *"The President of the United States."* At that time he brushed it off, but the dream became real not long after.

In 1912, many people reported uneasy dreams and warnings about the **Titanic**. A London newspaper collected letters after the tragedy, and dozens described family members who had begged loved ones not to board the ship because of terrible dreams. One man, Morgan Robertson, even wrote a novella in 1898 called *Futility*, about an "unsinkable" ocean liner called the *Titan* that struck an iceberg in the North Atlantic.

And it's not just big events. Ordinary people experience this, too. A mother in Ohio dreamt of her young son drowning in a neighbor's pool. The next day, shaken, she kept him home. That afternoon, when visiting the neighbor, she saw her toddler wander towards the pool's edge. She caught him just in time. To her, it wasn't a dream anymore, it was a warning.

Even science has nudged into this territory. In experiments at the **University of Nevada**, researchers found that participants' skin and heart rates sometimes shifted seconds before they were shown disturbing images, as if their bodies knew what was coming before their eyes did.

Stories like these raise a powerful question - "are premonitions just lucky guesses, or are they glimpses of timelines unfolding just ahead of us?"

Premonitions aren't necessarily about predicting doom or controlling the future. They may be subtle signals from your subconscious, from the fabric of time itself, or from something larger guiding you towards awareness.

When you get a strong intuitive nudge, it might be worth listening. Not in a fearful way, but as if life is whispering "*Pay attention. Something important is nearby.*"

If the universe really is layered with many possible futures, then your feelings and flashes of insight might be glimpses of those futures brushing against your awareness. **They don't lock you into a fate, they invite you to choose.**

PART 3

Harnessing Energy and Manifestation

Chapter 14

The Law of Attraction - Fact, Fiction, and Transformation

You've probably heard people talk about the Law of Attraction; it's everywhere - books, podcasts, social media videos. It has become one of those ideas that seem to pop up no matter where you turn. At its core, it's a pretty tempting promise - *what you focus on becomes your reality.* Think about money, love, or better health, and somehow the universe lines things up to match.

It's not hard to see why so many people get pulled in. Who wouldn't like the idea that life isn't just random; that you can guide it a little just by changing the way you think?

If you've ever felt stuck or powerless, that thought feels pretty comforting.

But, like most things that sound too easy, the truth isn't that simple. And honestly, that's what makes it worth looking at more closely.

The Law of Attraction resonates so deeply because, at the core of every person, there is a desire to know that life has meaning. Our thoughts and dreams are not idle wishes, but seeds of something real. People do not want to feel like leaves blowing aimlessly in the wind. They long to believe that their inner world shapes their outer world.

Like how your moods change what you see. When you are filled with love or enthusiasm, the world seems brighter. People smile back at you. Doors open where you once saw walls. But when you are discouraged or fearful, opportunities can be before your very eyes, and you will overlook them. The Law of Attraction expresses this simple truth that what you dwell on in your mind attracts its likeness in your experience.

Basically, what you focus on, you attract.

It is powerful because it restores a sense of authorship to your life. You are not a victim of chance or fate, you are a co-creator with the Infinite. Even if one does not accept every mystical claim made in its name, there is no denying the psychological and spiritual reality; your dominant thoughts guide your choices, influence others' responses, and set unseen forces in motion.

Think about this example - two people entering the same circumstance. One fills his mind with failure and limitation, and his actions echo that belief. The other quietly affirms harmony, success, and right action and he meets people and conditions that reflect this inner conviction. The outer world mirrors the inner world.

Ancient wisdom has whispered this for centuries: "As a man thinketh in his heart, so is he." The Law of Attraction is simply a modern phrasing of a timeless law of mind and spirit. Hold noble ideas, believe in them, and life begins to rearrange itself around those ideas.

The Law of Attraction has been sold in many places as something almost mechanical like - *"Visualize what you want, and the universe must give it to you."* People hear this, close their eyes, and spend a few minutes imagining riches, perfect health, or a dream partner. When nothing appears overnight, disappointment sets in.

This oversimplification causes two real problems. First, many people dismiss the entire idea as nonsense because it didn't work on command. They miss the deeper truth behind the principle. Second, and far more damaging, some begin to blame themselves when life takes a painful turn: *"Did I bring this illness on myself? Did I create this loss by thinking the wrong way?"* Such guilt is neither fair nor helpful. Life is far bigger and more complex than a single thought you had in a moment of doubt.

The Law of Attraction isn't about waving a magic wand, it's about the interplay between your inner world and the outer one. Your conscious thoughts plant seeds, but your **subconscious mind** tends the soil. You may consciously say, "I want abundance," but if you've been conditioned to believe you're unworthy or that money is always scarce, those hidden programs can block what you're trying to grow.

Real change happens when your conscious intention and subconscious beliefs move in the same direction and when you act on opportunities that align with them. For instance:

- A person might repeatedly visualize a healthier body but continue reinforcing stress and poor habits. Real alignment happens when they pair belief with small, consistent choices like nourishing food, gentle exercise, self-compassion.
- Someone might long for meaningful work but stay closed off to new connections or fear taking risks. When they start believing they *deserve* better, their confidence changes their actions. They network, apply, and notice doors that were always there but invisible before.

Timing also matters. Just as planting a seed doesn't yield a tree overnight, the results of your thoughts may need seasons to mature. The universe responds to persistence, patience, and readiness.

The Law of Attraction is not a vending machine where you insert a thought and instantly get a product. Your thoughts set the rhythm, your feelings give it energy, and your actions move you across. Life responds in kind, not always in the exact way you expect, but often in ways that surprise you with their wisdom.

Here's where things get really interesting. Science, in its own way, actually supports parts of the Law of Attraction.

Take the Reticular Activating System (RAS), your brain's filter for information. Tell yourself "I want a red car," and suddenly you start seeing red cars everywhere. They were always there, now your mind is tuned to notice them.

Or think about neuroplasticity, the brain's ability to rewire itself. Repeating new beliefs or visualizations literally strengthens neural pathways, making it easier to think, feel, and act in alignment with your goals.

Even emotions carry measurable energy. Studies show that positive emotional states like gratitude or love lower stress hormones and open creative problem-solving, while negative emotions narrow your focus to survival mode.

Science may not say, "Think of money and a suitcase of cash will land on your doorstep," but it *does* show that your focus changes your world in subtle, powerful ways.

Psychologists have found that when people hold a clear intention in mind, they unconsciously shift how they speak, stand, and make choices. Someone quietly committed to becoming healthier might not even realize they're taking the stairs more, ordering water instead of soda, or noticing an ad for a local fitness class they'd usually ignore. It's not magic, it's momentum.

Energy matters, too, in a very practical sense. Ever been around someone who's enthusiastic about a project? Their energy spreads, opening doors they couldn't have pushed alone. A study on "emotional contagion" showed that even a single optimistic person in a group can lift everyone's mood and performance. The reverse is true as well. Dwell in bitterness or fear, and you're less likely to see or act on the opportunities that could help you.

Seen this way, the Law of Attraction is less about commanding the universe and more about tuning yourself. By focusing on what matters, you not only notice more possibilities, you behave in ways that make them real. Over time, those small shifts create big changes that feel almost magical.

This is the part you rarely see on motivational posters or Instagram reels: thinking about something isn't enough. You can sit in your living room and repeat, *"I'm a best-selling author,"* a thousand times but if you never write a single page, there's nothing for the universe (or anyone else) to work with.

The real magic happens when belief, feeling, and action start moving in the same direction:

- **Belief** focuses your attention, so your mind starts spotting chances you'd normally miss.
- **Emotion** gives those beliefs power, signaling to your subconscious that this matters.
- **Action** anchors the idea in the physical world and creates momentum.

Think of it like planting a garden:

- **Visualization** is sketching out your dream garden on paper.
- **Affirmations** are the water and sunlight that keep your vision alive.
- **Action** is getting dirt under your fingernails - planting seeds, weeding, and tending the soil.

Without the last step, nothing grows.

That's why successful athletes, entrepreneurs, and creators pair mental rehearsal with relentless practice. The vision primes their brains to see possibilities, but it's the hours on the field, the pitches made, or the pages written that build the bridge between dream and reality. When your mindset and your actions align, opportunities don't just show up, they become something you're ready to step into.

So how do you make the Law of Attraction more than a daydream? The key isn't "forcing the universe" to give you things, it's aligning who you are with what you want.

That means shifting from vague wishing to believable, action-friendly statements. For example:

- Instead of saying, *"I want to be rich,"* you might say, *"I'm learning smart ways to manage money and build security."*
- Instead of *"I attract love,"* try, *"I'm growing into someone who gives and receives love with openness and kindness."*

This shift matters because your subconscious won't fully accept something that feels fake or impossible. But when your words match a path you can see yourself walking, your mind begins to treat it as real and starts looking for ways to support it.

It also keeps you grounded. You're not just sitting around waiting for magic; you're actively becoming the version of yourself who's ready for the life you want. Someone who builds skills, takes chances, meets new people, or shows up differently at work.

Transformation happens when belief, emotion, and action click into place; when what you say, how you feel, and what you do are all pointing in the same direction. That's when the "miracles" start to look a lot like you noticing opportunities you would've ignored before, and stepping through doors you might've been too scared to open.

So, is the Law of Attraction fact or fiction? The honest answer is - it's a little of both. The Hollywood version - the one where you just think about a sports car and it materializes in your driveway isn't how life works. But the deeper truth behind the idea is very real: what you consistently focus on changes what you notice, how you behave, the risks you're willing to take, and even the signals you send to other people. Over time, that focus shapes your reality in powerful ways.

Think about how many times a subtle shift in your mindset has already changed your day. Maybe you walked into a meeting confident instead of doubtful, and suddenly people responded differently. Or you decided to look for kindness instead of criticism, and almost magically you found it. That isn't coincidence; that's perception guiding experience.

The Law of Attraction isn't about bending the universe like a magic trick, it's about learning how your inner world creates ripples in the outer one. When your beliefs, emotions, and actions line up, you start to move through life differently. You notice doors you once overlooked. You take steps you once avoided. And because you're showing up in a new way, the world meets you in a new way too.

Harness that with clarity about what you want, genuine belief in your worth, and consistent action and you'll understand why this idea has captivated people across centuries. It's less about demanding miracles and more about becoming the kind of person who creates them.

Chapter 15

Energy Fields and Vibrations – The Science of Resonance

If you could shrink yourself down smaller than an atom and look closely at the world, you'd discover that nothing is ever completely still. The table under your coffee mug, the phone in your pocket, the ground beneath your feet, all of it is built from particles that are constantly moving. They're spinning, oscillating, and exchanging energy.

Even "empty" space isn't really empty. Physicists talk about the quantum vacuum, a sea of invisible energy where particles pop in and out of existence for the briefest moments. It's as if the universe is quietly humming under the surface, even when everything looks calm.

Everything Vibrates. Literally!

At every level of reality, movement and vibration are built-in. Electrons aren't sitting still around the nucleus of an atom; they're zipping around like tiny planets. Molecules don't stay frozen either, they bend, stretch, and wiggle every time they take in or release energy.

Even the Earth itself hums. Scientists call it the *Schumann resonance* - a low, steady vibration created by lightning strikes echoing through the Earth's atmosphere. Zoom way out, and entire stars pulse like cosmic heartbeats. Planets ring with their own frequencies, and galaxies swirl and spin like gigantic records in space. Zoom way in, and your own body is part of the same dance. Your heart cells send out rhythmic electrical pulses, your vocal cords vibrate to make sound, and even your DNA vibrates at specific frequencies.

You're not a static object walking through a silent universe, you're part of a constant, universal concert of motion and energy. Every breath you take, every thought you think, is happening in a world that's quietly buzzing all around you.

Now we'll head to the part where things get really interesting. Resonance happens when one vibration meets another and they start moving together in harmony. Think of a tuning fork. Strike one, and another fork with the same pitch across the room will start to hum on its own. The vibration has "jumped" across space and woken up something that was silent a moment before.

Resonance shows up everywhere. Soldiers are told to break stride when crossing a bridge, because if their marching matches the bridge's natural rhythm, the whole structure can start swaying dangerously and in rare cases, even collapse. Opera singers can shatter glass because their voice hits the exact frequency that the glass naturally vibrates at, pumping in energy until it gives way.

But resonance isn't limited to physics experiments or engineering mishaps. You've probably felt it in your own life. Ever walked into a room where everyone was laughing and, without even knowing why, you started smiling? Or met someone and instantly felt "in sync," as if you'd known them forever?

That's resonance too; not in the sense of shattering glass, but in the way emotions, moods, and energy can quietly tune in to each other.

Now, imagine scaling that idea up. If energy and vibration are part of everything, from molecules to planets, then resonance could be the invisible thread connecting not just objects, but experiences, people, and possibilities. It suggests that when your "frequency" - your mindset, emotions, or intentions matches something out in the world, you're more likely to notice it, connect with it, and bring it into your life.

Our body isn't just a bundle of organs wrapped in skin, it's an active electrical system. Every time our heart beats, it produces a small but measurable electromagnetic field. Your brain, too, is constantly firing off tiny electrical signals between billions of neurons. Doctors rely on machines like EKGs (to track your heart) and EEGs (to track your brain) to pick up these signals. In other words, you're buzzing with energy every second of your life.

The part most people don't realize is that your heart's field doesn't stay locked inside your chest. Experiments using sensitive instruments have detected the heart's electromagnetic field reaching several feet beyond the body. You may not see it or feel it directly, but it's there quietly pulsing into the space around you.

Think of times you've "felt" someone enter a room before you saw or heard them, or noticed how one person's mood can shift the atmosphere for everyone else. While science hasn't proven that this field carries emotions or thoughts, it does show we're not closed-off islands. On a very real, measurable level, your body radiates energy outward, and that energy is part of the invisible web connecting you to the world around you.

You've felt this, even if you didn't put words to it. You walk into a room where two people have just been fighting, and you instantly sense the tension. Before anyone says a word you can *feel* the heaviness in the air. No one tells you, your body picks it up.

Whereas, when you step into a lively party and your mood instantly lifts, even if you were tired a minute ago. Something in you tunes in and adjusts. The same thing happens on a bigger scale.

Think of a stadium concert when thousands of voices belt out the same chorus. The music isn't just sound at that point, it becomes a shared heartbeat. You don't have to know the people next to you to feel connected; the energy spreads and you find yourself moving with them.

This is resonance in action at the human level. Emotions aren't isolated private experiences; they're contagious. A grounded, calm person can bring stability to a tense group. One person's nervous energy can make a whole room uneasy. Your nervous system is constantly reading cues and syncing up with the emotional "frequency" around you; like - a glance, a shift in tone, a subtle tightening of shoulders. It's not magic; it's how humans evolved to survive and bond.

Long before science had machines to measure brain waves or terms like "resonance," people all over the world were already speaking the language of energy. In India, it was called *prana* - the life force that flows through everything. In China, it was *qi*, moving through invisible channels in the body. Many Native traditions talk about spirit energy, woven into the land, animals, and the natural cycles that sustain life. Different names, different images, but the same core idea. We are more than flesh and bone. We're currents of energy, connected to a larger flow.

For a long time, modern science dismissed these ideas as superstition. But lately, the gap between the mystical and the measurable has started to shrink. Researchers now study what they call *biofields* - subtle fields of energy that living beings generate. The heart and brain are the most obvious examples, but there may be more going on than just electricity. Some studies suggest these fields influence how our bodies heal, how we connect with others, and even how stress or calm spreads in groups.

Science doesn't yet have all the answers, it's just scratching the surface. But the fact that modern labs are even asking these questions shows how ancient intuitions weren't just poetic metaphors. They may have been pointing to something real all along; life isn't only mechanical, it's vibrational.

So what do you actually *do* with all this talk about energy and vibration?

The answer isn't about crystals or complicated rituals, it's about paying attention to what already affects you every day.

Think about how a single song can change your entire mood. A breakup ballad can leave you teary-eyed on your commute, while a favorite upbeat track makes you feel unstoppable. That's resonance!

Sound waves syncing with your emotions and shifting your internal state.

Breathing exercises, meditation, or yoga work in the same way. Slow, steady breathing can pull your nervous system out of stress mode and into calm. Chanting or drumming can settle racing thoughts or spark creative energy. Cultures all over the world have used rhythm and sound for centuries to guide the mind and body into balance, long before science could measure what was happening.

And it doesn't stop with music or movement. The people and places you surround yourself with are constantly tuning you. Hang out with someone who's enthusiastic and solution-focused, and you'll start to feel lighter and more motivated without even trying. Spend too much time around constant complaining or anger, and you'll feel drained.

Resonance isn't some mystical trick, it's a practical force shaping your mood, focus, and even your choices. The more intentional you are about what (and who) you tune into, the more you'll notice your own "frequency" shifting towards the life you actually want to live.

When you zoom out and really think about it, the idea is simple but huge. Nothing in this universe exists on its own or in isolation. You're not a sealed bubble floating through life untouched, you're part of a giant, connected web of vibrations, always sending and receiving energy.

Every thought you hold, every emotion you carry, even the way you walk into a room leaves a ripple. You're a living frequency. Once you understand that, you can start asking bigger questions!

Chapter 16

Synchronicity - Meaningful Coincidences and the Flow of Life

Have you ever suddenly thought of someone you haven't spoken to in years and then, almost immediately, your phone rings with that person on the line? Or maybe you've randomly opened a book, scrolled through an article, or met a stranger, only to find exactly the insight, idea, or answer you were looking for at that precise moment? These experiences make us stop in our tracks, smile, and wonder - is this really just coincidence, or is there something more at play?

Carl Jung gave these moments a name: **synchronicity**. He described them as meaningful coincidences. Events that aren't linked by simple cause and effect, but by significance. They carry a weight, an uncanny feeling that this isn't random, that the universe is somehow pointing you towards a particular insight, connection, or opportunity. Unlike everyday coincidences, which we might shrug off as chance, synchronistic moments have a way of grabbing our attention and leaving a lasting impression.

Synchronicity doesn't have to be some dramatic, life-changing miracle. More often, it whispers in small, subtle ways.

Maybe you miss your usual train and, instead of being annoyed, you stumble across a little café you've never noticed before. A week later, it becomes your favorite spot for coffee and quiet reflection.

Or perhaps a casual conversation with a stranger, someone you might have passed by without a second thought suddenly gives you the exact insight you needed for a decision you've been struggling with.

Sometimes it's even more subtle. The same number, phrase, or symbol keeps appearing in different contexts, almost as if the universe is tapping you on the shoulder, saying, "Pay attention here."

These moments are uncanny because they break the ordinary flow of life. They make you stop, even for a moment, and ask yourself: *How did that even happen?* They hint that life isn't just a sequence of random events, it's alive, responsive, and somehow aware of the journey you're on.

Sometimes life has a quiet way of guiding us; little signals that seem too precise to be mere coincidence. Imagine being at a crossroads, unsure which path to take. That was Mark's situation. He wandered into a bookstore, almost absentmindedly picked up a book, and began flipping through it. Then he came across a chapter that described, almost word for word, the steps he needed to take in his career. At the time, it felt like a coincidence. But looking back, he realized that moment had nudged him onto a path he might never have seen otherwise.

Or consider Sarah, sitting at a crowded airport, waiting for a delayed flight. She started a casual conversation with the person next to her. They exchanged ideas without any expectations. Months later, that same person became her partner in a project that transformed her career. It was a simple connection, but one that carried meaning far beyond that moment.

Even the smallest gestures can carry this invisible guidance. A man lost his wallet on a busy street and assumed it was gone for good. Days later, a stranger returned it to him with a note: "I felt like you needed this more than I did." That simple act didn't just restore his faith in humanity, it shifted his perspective on trust, generosity, and the decisions he made afterwards.

These stories have something in common. The inner and outer worlds aligning. When your mind, your attention, and your readiness are in harmony, life seems to respond in mysterious ways. Synchronicities are not just random events, they are whispers from the universe with gentle invitations guiding you along your path.

Have you ever noticed how certain moments seem perfectly timed, almost as if the universe paused just for you? That's the essence of synchronicity. Timing isn't random.

When your thoughts, intentions, and actions are aligned with your true purpose, or even just your deepest interests, your subconscious starts picking up tiny signals your conscious mind might miss.

These signals can be a subtle tone in someone's voice, a fleeting image, or even a number that keeps popping up. Somehow, they converge, nudging you toward insights, opportunities, or decisions that feel unnatural but not random.

It's a bit like tuning an old-fashioned radio. Most of the time, the station is there, but the static makes it hard to hear. When you adjust the dial just right, suddenly the music is clear, vibrant, and unmistakable. Synchronicity works the same way. When your inner "frequency" aligns with the world around you, life seems to arrange itself in meaningful patterns.

Of course, skeptics will say synchronicity is just coincidence - "you notice the hits and forget the misses." And yes, sometimes that's true. But it doesn't explain why certain coincidences hit so hard, carry emotion, or seem to repeat in patterns that are hard to ignore.

Some researchers suggest there might be more at play. Consciousness isn't strictly bound by the ticking of a clock. Your mind could be picking up signals, patterns, or possibilities that haven't fully materialized yet in linear time before they fully manifest. In Part 2, we looked at altered timelines and premonitions - moments where your awareness seems to stretch beyond the present. Synchronicity might be another way of experiencing that same truth that reality isn't just a straight line. It's layered, dynamic, and interconnected; and sometimes, if you're paying attention, the universe sends little markers to help you navigate it.

In other words, those meaningful coincidences might be less about chance and more about alignment. Your mind tuning into patterns that were already there, waiting to be noticed.

How to Invite Synchronicity Into Your Life

1. **Cultivate Presence** – Most synchronistic moments are subtle. If your mind is racing through worries, to-do lists, or distractions, you'll likely miss them. Being fully present, whether through meditation, mindful walking, or simply slowing down opens your awareness to little nudges and signals that might otherwise pass unnoticed.
2. **Follow the Nudges** – Sometimes a fleeting thought, a strange curiosity, or a gut feeling is more than random. It can be a doorway into a synchronistic experience. Maybe you feel drawn to read a certain book, make a call, or strike up a conversation. When you follow these small impulses, you create the conditions for meaningful coincidences to appear.
3. **Trust and Release** – Synchronicity doesn't respond well to control or force. Trying to manufacture coincidences usually leads to frustration. Instead, focus on aligning your inner world, your values, intentions, and mindset. When that alignment is in place, the right people, opportunities, and signs tend to show up naturally.
4. **Reflect** – Take time to look back at your experiences. Journaling synchronistic events can help you see patterns, connections, and recurring themes. Over time, you begin to notice how the universe or your mind's alignment with it is gently

guiding you, often in ways that make perfect sense in hindsight.

By practicing presence, following your instincts, trusting the process, and reflecting on the results, you start to move through life with an open hand rather than a clenched fist. And when that happens, synchronicity stops feeling like random luck and begins to feel like a conversation between you and the universe.

Think of synchronicity as gentle nudges from life itself, little signs showing you the way when you're paying attention. These moments remind us that life isn't just a string of random events. Opportunities, ideas, and people often appear exactly when they're meant to; not by luck, but because your inner world is quietly in tune with the flow around you.

When you start noticing these patterns, life begins to feel less like chaos and more like a guided journey. Doors open just as you're ready to walk through them. Solutions pop into your mind right when you need them. People cross your path at the perfect moment.

The secret isn't trying harder or forcing things to happen, it's aligning your thoughts, feelings, and intentions with the life you want. Trust that when your mind, heart, and actions are in harmony, the universe reflects that alignment back to you. Your inner frequency doesn't just influence your experience; it resonates with the larger flow of life, helping you move with guidance, ease, and purpose.

Chapter 17

Creative Visualization - Manifesting Through the Mind's Eye

Creative visualization isn't just idle daydreaming. It's a deliberate way of imagining the life, goals, or experiences you want **as if they're happening right now**. When you do this, you're training your mind to spot opportunities, sense possibilities, and guide your emotions and actions towards that vision.

Think of it like preparing for a big performance. An actor doesn't wait for opening night and hopes to "get it right." They rehearse, feel their role, and step into the character mentally again and again. Your brain works in much the same way. When you imagine an experience vividly, the same neural pathways activate as if the event was actually happening. Your emotions respond, your subconscious takes note, and your mind starts subtly adjusting your behavior to match the scene you're rehearsing.

The beauty of creative visualization is that it bridges imagination and reality. It primes your mind so that when real opportunities appear, you're ready to recognize them and act with confidence almost as if the universe has been preparing you for exactly that moment.

Do you know why *visualization* works?

The magic of creative visualization comes from how the brain handles imagination. Neuroscience tells us that when you picture yourself doing something vividly over and over, you're actually strengthening the same neural pathways you'd use if you were doing it in real life. Athletes, musicians, and performers have known this for decades: they mentally rehearse their routines, their bodies and minds follow that "mental blueprint," and when the real moment arrives, they perform with confidence and fluidity.

Visualization isn't just about perfecting a skill, it can shape your life. Your brain doesn't fully distinguish between a rich mental image and reality. The emotions you feel, the details you notice in your imagination, and the sense of "already being there" send signals to your subconscious. That part of your mind starts nudging your choices, actions, and attention in ways that make your imagined scenario more likely to become real.

It's subtle. You might start noticing opportunities you would have missed before, feel more confident in situations that once stressed you, or take actions that align with the life you've been visualizing, often without consciously realizing it. In short, your imagination becomes a rehearsal space for reality itself.

Creative visualization isn't just about picturing a goal in your mind, it's about *feeling* it too. Emotion is the fuel that brings your mental images to life. Excitement, joy, gratitude, and confidence turn a simple picture into something your mind and body can respond to as if it's real. Without that emotional spark, a vision is like a black-and-white photo. You can see it, but it doesn't move you or your life forward.

Think of it this way. Imagine you're visualizing finishing a big project. If you just see yourself holding the completed work, it's helpful but the real power comes when you feel the relief, pride, or excitement as if it's happening *right now*. That feeling tells your subconscious, "This is real. This matters." Suddenly, you start noticing opportunities you might have overlooked, your confidence rises, and your actions begin to line up naturally with the outcome you want.

Emotion is what makes the practice more than daydreaming. It's the difference between a still photo and a live movie in your mind; one that can subtly guide your choices, your energy, and even the way people respond to you. The more vividly you feel it, the stronger the ripple effect in your life.

Practical Steps for Daily Visualization

1. **Create a Quiet Space** - You don't need a meditation room or hours of free time. Even five minutes in the morning before your day starts, or in the evening before bed, can work wonders. Find a spot where you won't be interrupted, take a few deep breaths, and let your mind settle. This is your "mental rehearsal stage," where the real work begins.
2. **Focus on Specific Outcomes** - The brain responds to detail. Saying, "I want success" is too vague. Instead, paint a clear picture like - "I see myself confidently presenting my ideas to a room full of engaged listeners, receiving nods and smiles of approval." The more concrete your visualization, the easier it is for your mind to treat it like a real scenario and guide your actions towards it.
3. **Engage All Senses** - Don't just see it. Hear it, feel it, even smell it if possible. Imagine the sound of applause, the texture of a handshake, the excitement tingling through your body. Multi-sensory visualization makes the experience richer and more convincing for your subconscious.
4. **Feel It Deeply** - Emotions are the secret sauce. Allow yourself to experience the joy, pride, or relief of achieving your goal as if it's happening now. Don't force it; let it arise naturally. Your mind remembers emotions more strongly than images alone, and those feelings help anchor the vision in reality.

5. **Repeat Consistently** - Just like physical exercise or practicing an instrument, the benefits of visualization compound with regularity. Five minutes a day can be more powerful than an hour once in a while. Daily repetition strengthens the neural pathways in your brain, aligning your thoughts, feelings, and actions with your vision.

Creative visualization works best when it's more than just a mental exercise. The more clearly you see your goal, and the more feeling you pour into it, the more your thoughts, habits, and decisions naturally line up with that vision.

It's not magic, it's cause and effect. Your mind starts to notice opportunities you might have missed, nudges you towards helpful choices, and fuels the confidence to take action. Slowly but surely, what began as a picture in your mind begins to appear in your life. Visualization, when combined with intention and effort, transforms your inner world into a guiding force for your outer world.

PART 4

Beyond the Physical

Chapter 18

The Sixth Sense - Tapping into Hidden Perception

When people hear "sixth sense," they often picture crystal balls, fortune-tellers, or paranormal drama. But in reality, it's usually much more ordinary and far more practical than that. The sixth sense is simply heightened awareness. Your natural ability to pick up on information that doesn't arrive through sight, sound, touch, taste, or smell.

It's that subtle nudge (a quiet sense that something's off or right) before your logical mind catches up. Maybe you're interviewing candidates for a job and, despite the flawless résumé in front of you, something about one applicant's energy makes you hesitate… and months later you learn they weren't a good fit elsewhere. Or you're choosing between two apartments that seem identical on paper, but one just "feels" better and later you discover the other had hidden issues with noise or maintenance.

Sometimes it shows up in small, almost imperceptible ways. You pause before sending a text that might escalate an argument, or you sense the mood in a room shift before anyone says a word. None of these require psychic powers. Your mind is quietly piecing together micro-expressions, tonal shifts, and patterns from your experience. By the time you consciously register it, your intuition has already done the math.

Science offers some clues here. Your nervous system is constantly scanning for patterns - tiny changes in facial expression, tone of voice, body language, even shifts in air pressure or subtle environmental details. Your conscious mind can't juggle all this data at once, so much of it gets processed beneath the surface. What bubbles up is a "knowing" that feels instantaneous.

The sixth sense isn't about supernatural powers, it's about tuning into the signals already around you. The more you notice and trust these signals, the sharper and more reliable your intuition becomes. It's like a muscle; use it gently but consistently, and over time, you'll begin to sense opportunities, warnings, and connections that once seemed invisible.

Chapter 3 examined intuition's mechanics and its link to the subconscious. Here, the point is only this - intuition is one face of the sixth sense. It's the outcome you experience when many tiny signals - body sensations, context cues, memories, and probabilities are blended by your mind into a single, felt sense. We won't re-tell the same stories; instead, we'll widen the lens to include body-based sensing, environmental signals, and measurable physical fields that help explain how the sixth sense operates.

The sixth sense often speaks in whispers through dreams, flashes of imagery, or sensations in your body. Maybe you've woken up with a strange, vivid dream and brushed it off, only to see a detail from it show up later that day. Or you've felt an unshakable twinge of dread or excitement for no clear reason and then events unfolded in a way that matched that feeling.

These moments aren't always random. Researchers are discovering that your nervous system, heart, and even the cells in your body process far more information than your conscious mind can handle. Sometimes, those hidden signals surface as a nudge or a hint; a preview of a pattern that hasn't fully revealed itself yet.

While some people seem naturally intuitive, the sixth sense can be strengthened. The key is attention: noticing, reflecting, and trusting subtle impressions. Practices like mindfulness, meditation, journaling, or simply pausing to observe feelings and coincidences can sharpen your awareness.

For instance, try this exercise - before making a decision, sit quietly, close your eyes, and ask your subconscious what feels right. Notice the first images, sensations, or thoughts that arise. They may be subtle, but over time, these quiet nudges become reliable guides.

What makes the sixth sense truly fascinating is that it points toward something larger than our everyday experience. Intuition, premonitions, and subtle awareness suggest that consciousness may not be limited to the five senses and may reach beyond ordinary time, space, and sensory limitations. Your mind might be picking up signals from layers of reality that science is only beginning to understand; the same layers that could explain altered timelines, synchronicity, or even near-death experiences.

As you begin to notice these signals more, life can start to feel less rigid and predictable. You'll see patterns where others see chaos, sense opportunities before they appear, and feel a flow beneath the surface of daily events. It's not magic, it's a deeper tuning into the way reality moves, and learning to navigate it can give your decisions, creativity, and intuition a new kind of clarity.

The sixth sense is more than a curiosity. It's a bridge between the world we see and the hidden layers of reality. In the next chapter, we'll explore how physics and consciousness might actually be connected, revealing that intuition, perception, and the very fabric of reality could be intertwined in ways that challenge everything we thought we knew. By tuning into your hidden perception, you're already taking the first steps towards navigating a reality far richer than what your five senses can detect.

Chapter 19

Quantum Mind (Bridging Physics and Consciousness)

Modern physics reveals a universe far stranger than we usually imagine. At the tiniest scales, particles can exist in multiple states at once, influence each other instantly across vast distances, and even behave differently depending on whether they're being observed. In other words, the act of observing something can actually affect how it behaves.

This isn't just a weird scientific detail, it has real implications for consciousness. If reality at its core is probabilistic and interconnected, maybe the mind isn't limited to a purely mechanical body. Perhaps our awareness can actually interact with the underlying quantum fabric of the universe, influencing possibilities in ways we're only beginning to understand.

One of the most intriguing discoveries in quantum physics is the "observer effect." In simple terms, tiny particles behave differently when someone watches them. In the lab, this is measured with instruments, but it makes you wonder - "could our consciousness do more than just notice reality? Could it actually help shape it?"

Think of your mind as a lens. Out of all the possible ways a moment could unfold, your attention, intention, and focus might help "collapse" those possibilities into the version you experience. Every choice, every clear intention, even your focused thoughts could nudge which potential outcome becomes real. This idea lines up in surprising ways with intuition, premonitions, and creative visualization showing that the act of being aware might be more powerful than we ever imagined.

Imagine your brain not just as a biological computer, but as an instrument capable of tuning into subtle currents of reality. Deep inside each neuron are microscopic structures called **microtubules**, which some scientists believe could behave according to the strange rules of quantum physics.

If true, your brain may detect patterns, probabilities, or information that ordinary senses miss. That sudden insight, the unexpected solution to a problem, or a clear inner nudge could be your brain accessing possibilities beyond the linear, cause-and-effect world.

It doesn't mean your mind is magical, or that thought alone bends reality. Rather, consciousness might interact with the underlying fabric of reality in subtle ways, shaping the outcomes you notice and the decisions you make. Every intuitive pull, sudden clarity, or unexplained alignment may be your awareness catching glimpses of a more complex, interconnected reality.

Quantum entanglement reveals a remarkable property - two particles can remain connected so that a change in one instantly influences the other, regardless of distance. Now, imagine consciousness operating in a similar way. Your thoughts, emotions, or intentions might ripple out beyond your body, nudging situations, people, or even the environment in ways you don't fully notice.

This could help explain those moments when insight seems to appear out of nowhere, when you "just know" something about someone far away, or when a group of people suddenly share a synchronized idea or decision. It's as if our minds are part of a vast, unseen web; an interconnected network that quietly links each of us, much like entangled particles across the universe.

Even if we can't measure it directly yet, the concept hints at a profound truth that consciousness may be far more expansive and interconnected than we've been taught to believe.

Philosophers, mystics, and modern physicists all hint at a reality where consciousness and the physical world are deeply intertwined. Your awareness isn't just watching life unfold, it may be actively participating in it.

Exploring the quantum mind reveals that reality isn't a rigid stage where events simply happen to you. Instead, it's a dynamic field, constantly responding to intention, attention, and perception. Your consciousness is part of that field, subtly shaping the unfolding of events, guiding insights, and opening doors that might otherwise remain closed.

The next chapter takes this even further, showing what can happen when awareness moves beyond the body itself, pushing the limits of perception and exploring realms that challenge everything we think we know about life, death, and consciousness.

Chapter 20

Out-of-Body and Near-Death Experiences

Imagine lying in bed or in a hospital room and suddenly becoming aware that you are looking down at your own body from above. This is the core of an out-of-body experience (OBE) - a sense of consciousness existing independently from the physical body. People often describe floating, moving through walls, or traveling to distant locations in ways that defy ordinary physical limits.

Near-death experiences (NDEs) take this a step further. Those who have been clinically dead or close to it sometimes report traveling through a tunnel of light, encountering deceased loved ones, or feeling a profound sense of unconditional love and peace. These experiences are intensely real to those who live them, leaving lasting effects on their perception of life, purpose, and death.

Skeptics often suggest that out-of-body experiences (OBEs) and near-death experiences (NDEs) are simply the brain misfiring - hallucinations triggered by low oxygen, chemical changes, or unusual neural activity. And it's true that certain brain regions, such as the temporal lobe, show unusual activity during these events.

Yet what makes these experiences compelling is their remarkable consistency. Across different cultures, ages, and circumstances, people report similar sensations: floating above their bodies, moving through tunnels of light, or encountering beings of love and guidance. Such consistency challenges the idea that they are purely imagined or random.

Even more astonishing are cases where patients report accurate perceptions while the brain appears inactive. They describe events, conversations, or objects in the room that they could not have observed with their physical senses. These accounts suggest that consciousness may operate independently of the brain, hinting at a reality in which awareness is far more expansive than we typically assume.

What makes OBEs and NDEs fascinating is the way they challenge our assumptions about reality. If consciousness can exist independently of the body, even for a brief moment, it suggests that life might not be confined to the physical world. These experiences echo ideas from the quantum mind chapter: reality could be fluid, multi-layered, and deeply interconnected in ways we rarely perceive in our everyday lives.

Many who have experienced OBEs or NDEs describe a profound sense of unity with everything around them - a feeling of merging with universal awareness. Time and space seem to lose their usual meaning, and they gain a clarity about life, purpose, and connection that is difficult to describe. Some even say they intuitively understood how events, relationships, and choices in their lives are interwoven, almost like glimpsing the threads of a cosmic tapestry.

For others, the effects are more practical. After such an experience, decisions that once felt confusing or heavy suddenly feel clear. Priorities shift, relationships gain depth, and a renewed sense of gratitude or compassion emerges. In essence, OBEs and

NDEs don't just offer a glimpse beyond the physical, they can change the way a person navigates the physical world, aligning their inner awareness with a broader, more interconnected reality.

Whether you view these experiences spiritually or scientifically, they offer profound guidance:

- **Life is deeper than it seems:** There is more to existence than the physical senses can perceive.
- **Consciousness may transcend the body:** Awareness might be able to explore realms beyond ordinary space and time.
- **Perspective shifts:** Many people return with reduced fear of death, stronger empathy, and a clearer sense of purpose.

OBEs and NDEs invite us to question the boundaries of who we are. They suggest that consciousness isn't confined to neurons and tissue but may be an enduring, exploratory presence capable of interacting with realities beyond what we can see or touch.

For those who haven't had these experiences firsthand, the lessons still apply. These experiences highlight the vast potential of consciousness - the fact that awareness may extend beyond the physical body, perceiving patterns, connections, and possibilities that ordinary senses often miss.

Paying attention to your intuition, dreams, synchronicities, or those subtle nudges you sometimes get is like training your mind to notice the hidden layers of reality. Each time you follow a gut feeling, pause to reflect on a meaningful coincidence, or become aware of your inner guidance, you're practicing the same kind of awareness that people report at the edge of life.

In that sense, OBEs and NDEs aren't just extraordinary stories from rare moments, they're invitations. They encourage us to explore consciousness more fully, to trust our inner signals, and to live with a sense of connection to something larger than our immediate physical world. Integrating these lessons can help bring depth, clarity, and purpose to everyday life, long before any extraordinary event occurs.

PART 5

Transformation and Purpose

Chapter 21

Mind Over Matter - The Extraordinary Power Within

Most of us think of the mind as a passenger in life, reacting to circumstances rather than shaping them. But research and countless personal stories suggest the mind has far more influence than we commonly give it credit for. Thoughts, beliefs, and focused intention don't just stay in your head, they guide decisions, shape habits, and influence physical outcomes.

It's not magic. It's the real, practical power of focus, imagination, and belief working together. People who direct their attention and energy intentionally often recover faster, think more clearly, and even influence their physical health in measurable ways. Your mind isn't just watching life unfold, it's quietly helping create it.

Science has begun to uncover just how powerful this connection is. The placebo effect alone demonstrates that belief can trigger real biochemical changes in the body. Neuroplasticity reveals that the thoughts and actions we repeat actually rewire our brain, changing how we think, feel, and respond.

Stress, anxiety, or negative expectations influence hormones, immune function, and even cellular health. Conversely, focus, optimism, and visualization can improve resilience, learning, and performance.

Your mind is not a passive observer of your body, it's an active participant. Every thought, emotion, and intention creates ripples that reach far beyond your conscious awareness.

To harness this extraordinary power, you don't need esoteric rituals or mystical training. You start with simple, intentional practices:

- **Focused Attention:** Direct your thoughts and energy towards what you want to create, rather than what you fear or want to avoid.
- **Visualization:** Picture your goals vividly, engage your senses, and feel the emotions of success as if it's happening now.
- **Positive Belief:** Align your conscious mind with a belief that your efforts and intentions can influence reality.
- **Aligned Action:** Thoughts are powerful, but they work best when paired with deliberate action. Your mind prepares you to notice opportunities, while your efforts make them real.

We often go through life thinking that circumstances control us and life just **happens to us**. But the truth is: your mind quietly shapes your body, your habits, your emotions, and even the reality around you. Every thought, every intention, every moment you focus your attention is sending ripples into your world.

You don't need to attempt anything dramatic to notice it. It shows up in the little things like the way you calm yourself in a stressful moment by pausing and choosing how to respond; the way you imagine conversations going well before they even happen, and then they do; the way you gradually guide your habits by focusing on what you **want** instead of what distracts you. Each choice, each act of attention, is a small proof that mind over matter works; and over time, the results become unmistakable.

This isn't about forcing control over life. It's about realizing that you are more than your circumstances, more than the events swirling around you. Your inner world (your thoughts, your focus, your intentions) is constantly interacting with your outer world. Science shows it, experience confirms it, and when you notice it for yourself, the power you hold is no longer abstract or theoretical.

It's real. It's practical. It's ready to guide your life towards results you once thought were impossible!

Chapter 22

Life's Lessons - Patterns, Karma, and Cosmic Balance

Have you ever noticed how life has a way of repeating itself until we truly pay attention? Perhaps you find yourself struggling with a project at work, only to realize it feels eerily similar to a challenge you faced years ago. Or maybe certain types of people keep entering your life until you finally grasp what they're meant to teach you. These patterns aren't accidents; they're subtle signals from life nudging you towards awareness.

Sometimes these repetitions are quiet whispers - a friend who offers the same advice for the third time, a minor inconvenience that hints you might be going off course, a miscommunication that echoes a previous mistake. Other times, the lessons come crashing in, undeniable and unavoidable like a sudden loss, a major conflict, or a turning point that forces you to confront what you've been ignoring. These moments can feel frustrating or even unfair, but they are tailored to your growth, like a teacher who adapts the lesson until the student truly understands.

Think of life as a vast, intricate tapestry. At first glance, the threads may look chaotic, the colors random. But as you step back and pay attention, you begin to notice the patterns - threads looping back, echoes of earlier experiences, recurring themes that carry meaning. A failed relationship might later reveal what you truly value in a partner. A career setback might illuminate hidden strengths you didn't know you had. The same situations or challenges may appear in different forms, each time offering a deeper layer of insight.

The magic happens when you shift from frustration to curiosity. Instead of asking, "Why does this keep happening to me?" you can start to wonder, "What is life trying to show me?"

That subtle change in perspective transforms repetition from a source of annoyance into a guidepost. Life stops feeling like a series of random setbacks and begins to feel like a meaningful journey, where even missteps are part of the larger design.

Over time, noticing these patterns trains your awareness. You start to recognize subtle cues before events unfold, to see the lessons before they repeat, and to respond with greater clarity and wisdom. Life doesn't become perfectly predictable, but it does become more coherent. The same challenges appear less like obstacles and more like invitations to grow, adapt, and align with your true path.

Karma is one of those words that's often tossed around casually, sometimes as a joke, sometimes as a threat, as if the universe is waiting to hand out rewards or punishments. But at its heart, karma isn't about cosmic vengeance or divine favoritism. It's about cause and effect, the same principle that makes ripples when you toss a stone into water. Every thought, emotion, word, or action is a stone you cast, sending waves through your life and the lives of others.

These ripples don't always return instantly or obviously. Sometimes, the connection between cause and effect is crystal clear: you speak harshly in anger, and within moments, tension fills the room. But other times, the effects unfold quietly over weeks, months, or even years, weaving themselves into the larger story of your life. A pattern of kindness and integrity creates a gentle current in your favor, opening doors, strengthening bonds, and attracting experiences that reflect growth and trust.

On the other hand, fear, resentment, or selfish choices can create resistance, setting up situations that challenge you to reconsider your approach. This isn't punishment, it's feedback. Karma isn't keeping score like some cosmic referee; it's life responding to the energy you put out, offering chances to reflect, adjust, and grow.

Consider someone who repeatedly avoids responsibility or blames others. Life often brings them situations where accountability is unavoidable. Difficult bosses, broken relationships, financial crises - not because the universe is cruel, but because those experiences push them towards awareness and balance. Similarly, someone who chooses compassion, even in small ways, may notice opportunities and support flowing back to them in moments they least expect.

Seeing karma this way softens the sting of setbacks. A failed project isn't a sign that the universe is against you, it's information. A friendship drifting apart may be a nudge to reassess your boundaries or priorities. Even painful moments can reveal where your beliefs, choices, or actions are out of alignment with the flow of life.

As your awareness deepens, karma stops feeling like an external force acting on you and starts to feel like an ongoing conversation with life itself. The feedback becomes gentler because you don't need loud wake-up calls, you're already listening. And in that listening, you find freedom. The freedom to create new ripples with intention, to adjust your course, and to participate consciously in the ever-unfolding balance of the universe.

Life moves according to a deeper rhythm, even when, on the surface, everything seems uncertain. There is a balance operating quietly beneath your daily experiences - a give and take between effort and rest, challenge and blessing, loss and renewal. When you pause and reflect, you may recall moments when a closed door eventually revealed itself as a blessing in disguise, or when a delay led you to something far better than you had planned.

This is not an accident. The universe has a way of restoring harmony, even when your conscious mind cannot yet see the pattern. What appears as a setback may be a redirection. A painful ending may clear the path for a greater beginning. The gifts that arrive unexpectedly like the call from a friend just when you needed it, the sudden inspiration at the right moment are reminders that you are part of a greater flow of life.

Even in your quiet or lonely seasons, the rhythm is still at work. These pauses are not empty; they are spaces for renewal, preparing you for the next movement of growth. When you resist life's flow, you create tension and struggle. But when you trust its wisdom, when you align your thoughts, emotions, and intentions with its gentle current, you find a surprising ease.

Cosmic balance isn't a mystical concept. It reveals itself in the small acts of kindness you give and receive, in the lessons learned through both joy and hardship, and in the quiet knowing that nothing is wasted. When you open your heart to this truth, you begin to live with greater grace. You understand that every chapter, whether radiant or shadowed, belongs in the grand design of your growth. And with that understanding comes peace; the calm assurance that life's flow is always guiding you towards greater harmony, purpose, and fulfillment.

When you observe this flow, you begin to understand that every experience has a purpose, even those that seem painful or unfair. The key is to remain present, aware, and receptive, allowing life's natural cadence to shape your journey rather than resisting it.

When you step back from the day-to-day chaos, things start to make a little more sense. Events that once felt random like an unexpected setback, a chance meeting, or a sudden stroke of good luck can look like pieces of a bigger puzzle. Maybe a challenge you faced years ago shows up again, but this time you handle it with more patience and wisdom. Or someone from your past reappears just when their help or advice makes a difference.

It's almost as if life has a way of circling back, giving you the lessons you need until you truly get them. The universe doesn't waste experiences. The tough moments that shaped you, the small victories that encouraged you, even the gut feelings you almost ignored, they're all connected. Seeing life this way changes how you react.

This doesn't mean life will suddenly become predictable. There will always be surprises and mystery. But it does mean you can trust that even the hard parts have meaning. Karma isn't punishment, it's feedback. Patterns aren't traps, they're signposts. Challenges aren't enemies, they're opportunities to grow stronger and wiser.

The balance that holds everything together isn't mystical, it's right here, in your choices, your thoughts, and the kindness you show others. When you move with that flow instead of fighting against it, life starts to feel less like a series of random events and more like a meaningful journey. One that's been nudging you towards growth and understanding all along.

Chapter 23

Discovering Your Higher Purpose

There are moments when, right in the middle of an ordinary day, something quiet inside you asks, *"Is this all there is?"* It might come after a loss, during a big life change, or even just after reaching a goal you thought would finally make you happy. Maybe you've felt it while watching rain slide down a window, or lying awake in the stillness of night. Beneath the routine and the noise, there's a gentle pull; a whisper that your life is part of something greater.

This isn't a flaw or a sign of ingratitude. It's the deeper part of you stirring, reminding you that you were made for more than checklists and milestones. Everyone feels this at some point. Even those who seem to "have it all" eventually discover that money, recognition, or success are only chapters in a much bigger story and not the whole story itself.

We often picture "higher purpose" as something huge like starting a movement, saving the world, or leaving a legacy that makes headlines. But real purpose doesn't always shout. More often, it arrives quietly. It's the teacher who stays late to help a nervous student believe in themselves. It's the nurse who holds a trembling hand, or the friend who picks up the phone at just the right moment.

Think of the mechanic who fixes cars with honesty, knowing families trust him with their safety. Or the single parent who shows up every day, raising children with love and determination. These acts aren't small or unimportant, they're part of the invisible fabric that holds life together. When you bring care and intention even to the simplest task, you're already living with purpose.

Your higher purpose usually doesn't hit you all at once. More often, it shows up quietly, in little hints that guide you forward:

- The topics or causes that make your heart race when you talk about them.
- The problems, injustices, or situations that stir you to act or speak up.
- The talents or skills that feel natural to you, even when others struggle with them.
- The compliments or thanks people offer you, sometimes for things you barely notice you're doing.

Pay attention to these signs. They're like a gentle nudge, pointing towards where your natural gifts meet the world's needs. Often, what you dismiss as "just a hobby" or "no big deal" is actually a clue to your purpose.

Sometimes, your deepest sense of calling comes out of struggle. The person who lost a loved one to illness becomes an advocate for research. Someone who grew up with very little, works to create opportunities for kids in similar situations. A person who faced anxiety or depression trains to guide others through the darkness they once knew.

These transformations don't erase the pain, but they give it meaning. They show that even heartbreak can be fertile ground for growth, turning suffering into service, empathy, and understanding.

Often, the very experiences that challenged you most hold the key to the difference only you can make.

Purpose isn't something you stumble upon fully formed, it's something you grow into. Waiting for a perfect moment or a lightning-bolt revelation can keep you stuck. Instead, start where you are. Take small, meaningful steps today. A kind word, a creative project, or a first attempt at something you've always wanted to try.

With each step, clarity begins to build. You learn a little more about yourself, a little more about where your energy belongs. Your purpose takes shape not through waiting, but through doing.

Living with purpose carries a quiet power that often extends far beyond what you can see. You may never know how a single word comforted someone, or how a small act of courage inspired another to take a leap. An encouraging text, a shared story, or a simple moment of kindness can echo in ways you'll never witness.

The beauty of purpose is that it doesn't just fulfill you, it subtly shifts the world around you. When you live in alignment with what matters most, you enter a larger flow, and the impact multiplies in ways you can't predict.

Step back, and you may notice that your life has been preparing you all along. The detours, setbacks, victories, and moments of doubt, they're not random. They are threads weaving a bigger story.

Discovering your higher purpose isn't about chasing some perfect future. It's about recognizing that your life, exactly as it is today, already carries meaning. The world doesn't need another flawless hero, it needs you; living honestly, growing steadily, and sharing the gifts that only you can give.

CONCLUSION

Chapter 24

The Infinite Within

As we reach the final chapter, it's worth pausing to take in the journey we've traveled. From the subtle vibrations of the universe to the extraordinary power of the mind, from synchronicity and premonitions to the profound awareness of our higher purpose, we've explored layers of reality both seen and unseen. What emerges is a single, resonant truth which is - you are not a passive observer of life. You are an active participant, a conscious presence in a vast, intricate, and ever-unfolding tapestry.

The infinite within is not an imaginary concept. It is the awareness, energy, and potential that resides in every thought you have, every choice you make, and every interaction you engage in. It is the same force that allows intuition to guide you, that aligns your intentions with action, and that reveals patterns, lessons, and opportunities when you are willing to notice.

Mastery, in this context, is not about perfection or control. It is about understanding, aligning, and integrating. It is learning to navigate the physical, mental, and subtle realms with awareness and purpose. Every insight, every synchronicity, every step towards higher consciousness is a brushstroke on the canvas of your life. The more conscious you become of your inner world, the more skillfully you can shape your experience in the outer world.

Yet mastery alone is not enough. The other side of the infinite is mystery; the recognition that reality is far richer than our minds can fully comprehend. Quantum layers of existence, subtle fields of energy, and the unseen interconnectedness of life remind us that there will always be more to explore. Mystery keeps the journey alive; it humbles the mind while inspiring the heart. To integrate mystery with mastery is to live fully, embracing what you can understand, while remaining open to what transcends understanding.

In practice, this integration manifests as presence, choice, and alignment. You notice the thoughts that lift you, the feelings that guide you, and the opportunities that resonate with your inner truth. You act with intention, but without clinging, trusting that life responds to clarity and authenticity. You honor patterns and lessons, while remaining flexible to change. You nurture relationships, express creativity, and contribute in ways that matter. Not for recognition, but because your higher self knows its role in the grand design.

Ultimately, the infinite within is both **the source and the destination**. It is the spark that awakens curiosity, the force that fuels growth, and the quiet voice that whispers, *you are part of something greater*. By integrating what we've explored (mind, energy, perception, purpose, and connection) you step into life not as a spectator, but as a co-creator of your experience.

So as you close this book and return to your own journey, remember that the unknown is not a threat, and the extraordinary is not reserved for a chosen few. Every moment, every choice, every intention carries the power to expand consciousness, deepen understanding, and enrich the world. The infinite is not somewhere "out there", it has been within you all along, waiting for recognition, practice, and integration.

You are more than your circumstances. You are more than your thoughts. You are a living, breathing expression of mystery and mastery, continuously learning, evolving, and co-creating the reality in which you participate. The journey beyond the known has no final endpoint; it is, and always will be, the infinite unfolding within you.